LINCOLN CHRISTIAN COLLEGE AND SEMINARY

The State
of
Church Giving
through 1995

John L. Ronsvalle

Sylvia Ronsvalle

empty tomb, inc.
Champaign, Illinois

The State of Church Giving through 1995 by John and Sylvia Ronsvalle
published by empty tomb, inc.
First printing, December 1997
Second printing, August 1998

© Copyright, empty tomb, inc., 1997
This publication may not be reproduced in part or whole, in any form or by any means,
without prior written permission from empty tomb, inc.

empty tomb, inc.
301 North Fourth Street
P.O. Box 2404
Champaign, Illinois 61825-2404
Phone: (217) 356-9519
Fax: (217) 356-2344

ISBN 0-9639962-6-6
ISSN 1097-3192

Contents _____

Gratis

98043

Tables and Figures

Table of Contents

Preface

Without the committed efforts and cooperation of the denominational officials at all levels of the church, valuable information about church giving and membership patterns would go unrecorded. We want to acknowledge the labors of these individuals throughout this century. Their important work provides a basis for the historical analysis contained in this study.

We also acknowledge the commitment of the National Council of the Churches of Christ in the U.S.A. to publish the data. Under the leadership of Joan B. Campbell, General Secretary, and the Communication Commission, this organization has continued to play a major role in making this information available in a usable format to scholars and the general public through the *Yearbook of American and Canadian Churches* series.

Kenneth B. Bedell served as the editor of the *Yearbook* through the 1996 edition. His efforts during his tenure as editor are greatly appreciated, and we would note that it was a pleasure to work with him.

The other staff and those who support the works of empty tomb make a critical contribution to our ability to produce this series of church giving analyses. We are most grateful to them. In particular, we would like to thank Sarah Hartmann, who provided invaluable assistance in the production of this edition.

As the above paragraphs indicate, many people are involved in producing a report such as this one. Nevertheless, the authors take responsibility for the content on the following pages. The data supports the conclusion that church giving could improve from present levels. It is our hope that this report will provide information and assistance in challenging the church in the U.S. to fulfill more of its potential for sharing God's love with a hurting world in the name of Jesus Christ.

John L. Ronsvalle, Ph.D.
Sylvia Ronsvalle

Champaign, Illinois
December 1997

Summary

The State of Church Giving through 1995 is the most recent report in a series that considers denominational giving data for a set of denominations first analyzed in a study published in 1988. The present report reviews data for 29 denominations that include 30 million full or confirmed members, and just over 100,000 of the estimated 350,000 religious congregations in the U.S.

The findings of the present church member giving analysis include:

- Church giving, on a per member basis, increased from 1994 to 1995 in both current and inflation-adjusted dollars. Per member giving as a percentage of income declined to Total Contributions, and the two subcategories of Congregational Finances and Benevolences. Benevolences declined as a portion of income for the tenth year in a row. In 1995, if giving as a percentage of income had not declined but rather had been at the 1968 level, members would have donated $3.9 billion more than they did.

- When the composite group of 29 denominations was expanded to include 49 Protestant communions, and data was compared for 1994-1995, the decline in giving as a percentage of income to Benevolences was also evident in the expanded set.

- An analysis of data for a subset of mainline Protestant denominations and a subset of evangelical Protestant denominations found giving higher in the evangelical Protestant denominations, but a steeper decline in giving patterns among the evangelicals over the 1968-1995 period. Although the evangelical denominations were increasing in membership during these years, their members were giving a smaller contribution as a portion of income. The mainline denominations increased contributions as a percent of income to Congregational Finances between 1985 and 1995, while a continuing decline to Benevolences was evident.

- A review of giving patterns in 11 Protestant denominations from 1921 to 1995 found per member giving as a portion of income was above 3% from 1922 through 1933, the depth of the Great Depression. It declined in the following years, reaching a low point during World War II. Giving increased through the 1950s, reaching a post-war high of 3.15% in 1960. Giving as a portion of income began to decline in the early 1960s, predating many of the controversial issues often cited as reasons for declines in giving. The 1955-1960 period had the highest ratio of per member giving increase compared to per capita income increase, followed closely by 1950-1955. The 1947-1960 period was the longest sustained period of increase in per member inflation-adjusted dollars, followed by 1975-1995.

- Data for 1968-1985 was analyzed using both linear and exponential regression. Then 1986-1995 data was compared to the resulting trends. Benevolences as a portion of income more closely resembled the linear regression. Congregational Finances more closely resembled the exponential curve. Membership in 10 mainline denominations as a portion of U.S. population was best described by an exponential curve, while membership as a portion of U.S. population for the 29 denominations resembled the linear regression trend more closely. The potential for church giving levels was calculated: at the rate of income increase; on a trend that would reach 10% giving in the year 2050; and at 10% in 1995. The results suggested that church members have sizable resources available, in theory, to apply to domestic and global needs. However, the data in the earlier chapters suggests church members have displayed no signs of improving giving patterns.

- The annual rate of change in the data set of 29 denominations was used to develop a total giving to religion series keyed to the 1974 Filer Commission estimate of giving to religion. This series was compared to the American Association of Fund Raising Counsel, Inc. (AAFRC) *Giving USA* series. The AAFRC series includes data for years when AAFRC added to religion any difference between their total giving estimate and the sum of its use category estimates. The AAFRC series was higher than the denomination-based series. This finding had implications for individual giving and total giving, since giving to religion was over 55% of individual giving. The AAFRC data also differed from the Independent Sector *Giving and Volunteering in the United States* series. External validation was used to compare the Independent Sector data with other sources of information. The Independent Sector data varied at key points from the external data.

- A review of classical church documents, written by Martin Luther and John Calvin, as well as more contemporary sources, affirm the traditional position of justification by faith. In addition, the same sources support the conclusion that faith should be evident in the behavior of those who profess to believe. The declining church giving patterns suggest, in this context, that there are church members whose behavior would indicate that they do not have faith to accompany their confessions, and therefore could be at risk of not going to heaven but instead of going to hell.

Introduction

On the following pages is an analysis of data that has been provided by approximately 100,000 congregations operating throughout the United States. Given that there are an estimated 350,000 religious congregations of any type in the U.S., the following aggregated information provides an important indication of how church members value their religious affiliation, as evidenced in giving patterns.

The individual congregations initially provided the data to the regional or national denominational office with which the congregation is affiliated. The denominational offices then compiled the data and published it in annual reports. The *Yearbook of American and Canadian Churches* (*YACC*), of the National Council of the Churches of Christ in the U.S.A., requested and compiled this data from the national denominational offices, publishing it in the annual *YACC* editions.

The data published by the *YACC*, in some cases combined with data obtained directly from a denominational source (as noted in the series of tables in Appendix B), serves as the basis for the present report.

A comparison of data for a given set of denominations over a period of years permits a review of patterns in giving. This denominational giving composite may also be used to compare subsets of denominations based, for example, on theological perspectives as self-identified by denominations' affiliation with national organizations.

Several analysis factors have been revised in *The State of Church Giving through 1995* (see the section titled "Revised Analysis Factors" below).

Definition of Terms. The analyses in this report use certain terms that are defined as follows.

Full or Confirmed Members are used in the present analysis because it is a relatively consistent category among the reporting denominations. Certain denominations also report a larger figure for Inclusive Membership, which may include, for example, children who have been baptized but are not yet eligible for confirmation in that denomination. In this report, when the term "per member" is used, it refers to Full or Confirmed Members, unless otherwise noted.

Total Contributions Per Member refers to the average contribution in either dollars or as a percentage of income which is donated to the denominations' affiliated congregations by Full or Confirmed Members in a given year.

Total Contributions combines two subcategories. The definitions used in this report for the two subcategories are consistent with the standardized *YACC* data request questionnaire.

The first subcategory is Congregational Finances, which includes all contributions directed to the internal operation of the individual congregation, including such items as the utility bills and salaries for the pastor and office staff, as well as Sunday school materials and capital programs.

The other subcategory is Benevolences. This category includes contributions for the congregation's external expenditures, beyond its own operations, for what might be termed the larger mission of the church. Benevolences includes international missions as well as national and local charities, through denominational channels as well as programs of nondenominational organizations to which the congregation contributes directly. Benevolences also includes support of denomination administration at all levels, donations to denominational seminaries and schools. It may be noted that in the case of one denomination considered in chapters two and four, the category includes pastoral medical insurance and pension payments.

When the terms "income," "per capita income," and "giving as a percentage of income" are used, they refer to the U.S. Department of Commerce Bureau of Economic Analysis' U.S. Per Capita Disposable (after-tax) Personal Income series, unless otherwise noted.

The Implicit Price Deflator for Gross National Product was used to convert current dollars to 1992 dollars, thus factoring out inflation, unless otherwise specified (see "Revised Analysis Factors" section below).

Appendix C includes both U.S. Per Capita Disposable Personal Income figures and the Implicit Price Deflator for Gross National Product figures used in this study.

Revised Analysis Factors. In October 1995, the U.S. Bureau of Economic Analysis (U.S. BEA) issued revised tables for implicit price deflators. These tables were part of a comprehensive revision that affected three factors used in *The State of Church Giving* series: deflators, chained dollars, and income series. As a result, the analyses in *The State of Church Giving through 1995* revise and update findings in the earlier editions.

Deflators. Past editions in *The State of Church Giving* series used the Implicit Price Deflator for National Income. The U.S. BEA does not currently publish this series.[1] Therefore, the Implicit Price Deflator for Gross National Product series will be used.

Chained Dollars. The U.S. BEA issued a comprehensive revision, including a change from "constant 1987 dollars" to "chained (1992) dollars." The revised figures provide " 'chain-type annual-weighted' measures."[2] The benchmark year was changed from 1987 to 1992 "because that is the latest year for which the current-dollar estimates will not be subject to revision until the next comprehensive revision."[3]

---

[1] *Survey of Current Business*, October 1995, page 39.

[2] *Survey of Current Business*, October 1995, page 30.

[3] *Survey of Current Business*, October 1995, page 30, footnote 3.

Income Series. The U.S. BEA is in the process of publishing a revised income series, in conjunction with its comprehensive revision. The U.S. Per Capita Disposable Personal Income data used in the present *The State of Church Giving through 1995* includes a 1929-1958 series received from the U.S. BEA Personal Income Division in a fax dated June 17, 1997, and a 1959-1996 series received in a June 16, 1997 fax from the U.S. BEA Personal Income Division.

Revised Calculation, 1985-1995. In past reports, the rate of change for 1968-1985 and 1985 through the most recent report year were calculated from the 1968 and 1985 base years, respectively. However, it became clear that an acceleration was thereby introduced in the post-1985 data set.

Therefore, *The State of Church Giving through 1995* employs the following methodology to calculate the rate of change between 1985 and the most recent calendar year, which in the present case is 1995.

As was the case in previous editions, the rate of change between 1968 and 1985 is calculated by subtracting the 1968 giving as a percentage of income figure from the 1985 figure and then dividing the result by the 1968 figure.

However, in the current edition, the rate of change between 1985 and 1995 is calculated as follows. The 1968 giving as a percentage of income figure was subtracted from the 1995 figure and divided by the 1968 figure, producing a 1968-1995 rate of change. Then, the 1968-1985 rate of change was subtracted from the 1968-1995 figure. The result is the 1985-1995 rate of change, which may then be compared to the 1968-1985 figure.

Rounding Calculations. In most cases, Total Contributions, Total Congregational Finances and Total Benevolences for the denominations being considered were divided by Full or Confirmed Membership in order to obtain per capita, or per member, data for that set of denominations. This procedure occasionally led to a small rounding discrepancy in one of the three related figures. That is, by a small margin, rounded per capita Total Contributions did not equal per capita Congregational Finances plus per capita Benevolences. Similarly, rounding data to the nearest dollar for use in tables and graphics led on occasion to a small rounding error in the data presented in tabular or graphic form.

Giving in Dollars. Per member giving to churches can be measured in dollars. The dollar measure indicates, among other information, how much money religious institutions have to spend. Did congregations have as much to spend in 1995 as they did in 1968? This question can be considered in both current dollars and inflation-adjusted dollars.

Current dollars indicate the value of the dollar in the year it was donated. However, since inflation changes the value of the dollar, data provided in current dollars has limited information value over a time span. If someone donated $5 in 1968 and $5 in 1995, on one level that person is donating the same amount of money. On another level, however, the buying power of that $5 has changed a great deal. Since less can be bought with the $5 donated in 1995 because of inflation in the economy, on a practical level the value of the donation has shrunk.

To account for the changes caused by inflation in the value of the dollar, a deflator can be applied. The result is inflation-adjusted 1992 dollars. Dollars adjusted to their chain-type, annual-weighted measure through the use of a deflator can be compared in terms of real growth over a time span since inflation has been factored out.

The deflator most commonly applied in this analysis designated the base period as 1992, with levels in 1992 set equal to 100. Thus, when adjusted by the deflator, the 1968 gift of $5 was worth $18.08 in inflation-adjusted 1992 dollars, and the 1995 gift of $5 was worth $4.65 in inflation-adjusted 1992 dollars.

Giving as a Percentage of Income. There is another way to look at church member giving. This category is giving as a percentage of income. Considering what percentage or portion of income is donated to the religious congregation provides a different perspective. Rather than indicating how much money the congregation has to spend, as when one considers dollars donated, giving as a percentage of income indicates how the congregation rates in light of church members' total available incomes. Has the church sustained the same level of support from its members in comparison to previous years, as measured by what portion of income is being donated by members from the total resources available to them?

Percentage of income is a valuable measure because incomes change. Just as inflation changes the value of the dollar, so that $5 in 1968 is not the same as $5 in 1995, incomes, influenced by inflation and real growth, also change. For example, per capita income in 1968 was $3,101 in current dollars; if a church member gave $310 that year, that member would have been tithing, or giving the standard of ten percent. In contrast, 1995 per capita income had increased to $20,214 in current dollars; and if that church member still gave $310, the member would have been giving only 1.5% of income. The church would have commanded a smaller portion of the member's overall financial activity.

Thus, while dollars donated indicate how much the church has to spend, giving as a percentage of income provides some measure of the level of commitment the church member displays for the church in comparison to the church member's total spending. One might say that giving as a percentage of income is an indication of the church's "market share" of church members' lives.

In most cases, to obtain giving as a percentage of income, total income to a set of denominations was divided by the number of Full or Confirmed Members in the set. This yielded the per member giving amount in dollars. This per member giving amount was divided by per capita income. Disposable personal income was used since this after-tax figure eliminated the variation in taxes paid during any time period under consideration.

Data Appendix and Revisions. Appendix B includes the denominational data used in the analyses in this study. In general, the data for the denominations included in these analyses appears as it was reported in editions of the *YACC*. In some cases, data for one or more years for a specific denomination was obtained directly from the denominational office or another denominational source. Also, the denominational giving data set has been refined and revised as additional information has become available. Where relevant, this information is noted in the appendix.

1

Church Member Giving, 1968-1995_____

Americans were more health conscious, more educated and entertained themselves more in the mid-1990s compared to the late 1960s.

For example, Americans ate 15% less red meat on average, consuming 112 pounds in the mid-1990s compared to 132 pounds a year as the 1960s closed. Meanwhile, chicken-eating increased by 72%, from 27 to 47 pounds per year. During this period, Americans increased their consumption of lowfat milk and yogurt, cut back on sugar and increased consumption of corn sweeteners. Meanwhile, mushroom eating grew from 1.3 to 3.9 pounds a year, an increase of 200%. And while the population increased by 27% from the late 1960s to the 1990s, the percentage of the population that smoked decreased from over 46% to 27%.

Perhaps some of these lifestyle changes contributed to the fact that life expectancy increased from 70.8 years to 76.3.

Americans were more educated as well. More people completed high school and more went on to college. Even so, the number of people who read a newspaper stayed about constant. Taking the growth in population into account, a smaller portion of citizens were getting their news from the daily printed page.

The entertainment industry boomed, with per capita expenditures growing by 165%. Almost two-thirds of the U.S. had cable television by the mid-1990s, compared to only 7% in 1970. While VCRs did not exist in the late 1960s, 79% of the population had one by 1994.

Not all the increases were constructive, though. The percentage of the population in jail also changed in this period. In 1970, there were 0.96 inmates per 1,000 of U.S. population serving sentences of over one year, compared to 3.53 in 1993.

This data suggests that alterations in lifestyle can be seen as improvements or declines in the quality of life—or merely as changes in behavior patterns. Studying changes in church member giving patterns during the period of the late 1960s through the mid-1990s can also give us insight into Americans' behavior patterns. If one sees the church as a constructive social institution, improvements in giving would be seen as a positive development, while declines in giving would be a cause for concern. If one had no value judgment about the church as a social institution, changes in giving would still provide insight into Americans' priorities, as indicated by how they distributed their resources in light of their professed religious affiliation.

Twenty-nine Denominations. The present report is the eighth in a series that has tracked giving patterns in a set of Protestant communions in the U.S. that span the theological spectrum. The first study in the present series was published in 1988. It considered a set of 31 denominations which provided church member giving data for 1968 and 1985 in the *Yearbook of American and Canadian Churches (YACC)* series that could be confirmed.[1] The data year 1968 was selected because, beginning that year, a consistent distinction was made between Full or Confirmed Membership and Inclusive Membership in the *YACC* series. The denominations that published data for both 1968 and 1985 included 29,442,390 Full or Confirmed Members in 1985. They comprise approximately 100,000 of the estimated 350,000 religious congregations in the U.S.

Following editions in the church member giving report series extended the analysis for the original set of denominations beyond 1985. The current report analyzes the data set, now comprising 29 denominations, through 1995, the most recent year for which data was available at the time the report was written.[2] Also, data for the intervening years of 1969 through 1984 was included in the composite data set, as available.[3]

Church member giving can be considered from two perspectives. One might discuss the number of dollars a member gives to the church. The second approach would be to consider the portion, or percentage, of income that members donate to the church. The data yields the following observations for the denominations considered in this analysis.

Church Giving in Current Dollars. The number of dollars donated to a church are of interest because this factor considers how much the church, as a social institution, has to spend. Calculating contributions on a per member basis accounts for changes in membership, either through growth or decline, that might have taken place during the period under review. The number of dollars donated by members indicates how much the church had to spend on both local institutional operations as well as what might be termed its larger mission.

When considering the number of dollars donated, there are, in fact, two aspects to this category: current dollars (the value the dollars had in the year they were donated); and inflation-adjusted dollars.

---

[1]John Ronsvalle and Sylvia Ronsvalle, *A Comparison of the Growth in Church Contributions with United States Per Capita Income* (Champaign, IL: empty tomb, inc., 1988).

[2]Two of the original 31 denominations merged in 1987, bringing the total number of denominations in the original data set to 30. As of 1991, one denomination reported that it no longer had the staff to collect national data, resulting in a maximum of 29 denominations from the original set which could provide data for 1991 through 1995. Therefore, throughout this report, what was an original set of 31 denominations in 1985 will be referred to as a set of 29 denominations, reflecting the denominations' 1995 composition, although data for 31 denominations will be included for 1968 and 1985, as well as for intervening years, as available.

[3]For 1986 through 1995, annual denominational data has been obtained which represented for any given year at least 99.52% of the 1985 Full or Confirmed Membership of the denominations included in the 1968-1985 study. The number of denominations for which data was available varied from a low of 25 in 1986 to a high of 29 in 1991 through 1995. The denominational giving data considered in this analysis was obtained either from the *Yearbook of American and Canadian Churches* series, or directly in correspondence with a denominational office. For a full listing of the data used in this analysis, including the sources, see Appendix B-1.

Table 1 presents the data for the per member contribution in dollars for the composite group of denominations included in the data set. The data is considered in three categories. Total Contributions Per Member represents the average total contribution for each full or confirmed church member in the composite of 29 denominations. This Total Contributions figure is comprised of two subcategories: Congregational Finances (which includes the monies the congregation spent on internal operations); and Benevolences (which includes what might be termed the larger mission of the church, such as local, national and international missions, as well as denominational support and seminary funding, among other items).

Table 1: **Per Member Giving to Total Contributions, Congregational Finances and Benevolences, Current and Inflation-Adjusted 1992 Dollars, 1968-1995**

	Per Full or Confirmed Member Giving to Congregations, in Dollars								
	Current Dollars			Inflation-Adjusted 1992 Dollars					
Year	Total	Cong. Finances	Benevol.	Total	↑↓	Cong. Finances	↑↓	Benevol.	↑↓
1968	$96.58	$76.21	$20.37	$349.17		$275.54		$73.63	
1969	$100.63	$79.03	$21.60	$347.47	↓	$272.89	↓	$74.58	↑
1970	$103.82	$82.57	$21.25	$340.40	↓	$270.73	↓	$69.66	↓
1971	$109.43	$86.92	$22.51	$341.13	↑	$270.96	↑	$70.17	↑
1972	$116.91	$93.08	$23.83	$349.62	↑	$278.35	↑	$71.27	↑
1973	$127.23	$101.87	$25.36	$360.23	↑	$288.42	↑	$71.81	↑
1974	$138.74	$110.64	$28.10	$360.45	↑	$287.44	↓	$73.00	↑
1975	$149.93	$118.17	$31.76	$356.05	↓	$280.62	↓	$75.43	↑
1976	$162.63	$128.88	$33.75	$364.81	↑	$289.10	↑	$75.72	↑
1977	$175.40	$139.79	$35.61	$369.57	↑	$294.53	↑	$75.04	↓
1978	$192.57	$154.26	$38.31	$378.19	↑	$302.95	↑	$75.24	↑
1979	$211.15	$169.17	$41.98	$382.10	↑	$306.13	↑	$75.97	↑
1980	$231.90	$185.59	$46.32	$384.20	↑	$307.46	↑	$76.74	↑
1981	$255.08	$203.96	$51.12	$386.19	↑	$308.80	↑	$77.39	↑
1982	$275.73	$223.22	$52.51	$392.72	↑	$317.93	↑	$74.78	↓
1983	$292.62	$236.47	$56.15	$399.75	↑	$323.05	↑	$76.70	↑
1984	$315.34	$256.34	$59.01	$415.09	↑	$337.42	↑	$77.67	↑
1985	$335.63	$272.55	$63.08	$427.17	↑	$346.89	↑	$80.28	↑
1986	$352.84	$287.50	$65.33	$437.66	↑	$356.61	↑	$81.04	↑
1987	$367.23	$300.67	$66.57	$441.97	↑	$361.86	↑	$80.12	↓
1988	$381.92	$312.13	$69.79	$443.48	↑	$362.44	↑	$81.04	↑
1989	$403.02	$330.18	$72.84	$449.05	↑	$367.89	↑	$81.16	↑
1990	$419.52	$345.53	$73.99	$448.06	↓	$369.04	↑	$79.03	↓
1991	$433.69	$357.96	$75.73	$445.59	↓	$367.78	↓	$77.81	↓
1992	$445.16	$367.42	$77.74	$445.16	↓	$367.42	↓	$77.74	↓
1993	$457.72	$379.82	$77.91	$446.08	↑	$370.15	↑	$75.93	↓
1994	$477.21	$396.99	$80.22	$454.74	↑	$378.30	↑	$76.44	↑
1995	$498.20	$415.52	$82.68	$463.10	↑	$386.24	↑	$76.86	↑

Details in the above table may not compute to the numbers shown due to rounding.

During the period 1968 through 1995, the per member amount given to Total Contributions increased in current dollars each year. The part of Total Contributions Per Member which stayed in the congregation to fund Congregational Finances also went up each year. Per member contributions in current dollars directed to Benevolences also increased each year between 1968 and 1995, except from 1969 to 1970, when there was a decrease of $0.35.

Overall, Total Contributions to the church in current dollars increased $401.62 on a per member basis from 1968 to 1995. Of this amount, $339.31 was directed to increase the per member Congregational Finances expenditures, for the benefit of members within the congregation. That allocation meant that $62.31 more per member was available to increase the Benevolences, or outreach, activities of the congregation.

At first glance, one might conclude from these figures that church member giving increased at a reasonable rate from the late 1960s to the mid-1990s. However, in order to understand how much a congregation's purchasing power had increased, these donations should be reviewed once more after inflation has been factored out.

Church Giving in Inflation-Adjusted Dollars. The U.S. Bureau of Economic Analysis (U.S. BEA) periodically revises the deflator series that are used to factor out inflation, thus allowing dollar figures to be compared across years. The U.S. BEA issued such a revision in the mid-1990s. The year of base comparison was changed from 1987 to 1992. Further, a change was made from the concept of "constant" dollars to "chained" dollars.[4] By applying the revised implicit price deflator to the current dollar church member giving data, the data can be reviewed across years with inflation factored out. The result of this process is also listed in Table 1.

Once the effects of inflation are removed, a different pattern in church member giving is observed.

Per member contributions to Total Contributions increased in the majority of years. The only years that posted declines were in 1969, 1970, 1975, and a three-year period from 1990 to 1992.

Congregational Finances increased from one year to the next except in six years— 1969, 1970, 1974, 1975, and a two-year period from 1991 to 1992—when per member contributions in inflation-adjusted 1992 dollars decreased from the previous year.

Benevolences also increased in the majority of years. Decreases may be observed eight times in the 1968-1995 interval, in 1970, 1977, 1982, 1987, and a four-year period from 1990 to 1993.

Figure 1 presents the changes in inflation-adjusted dollar contributions to the three categories of Total Contributions, Congregational Finances and Benevolences.

What changes occurred overall during this period, once inflation was factored out? Per member donations to Total Contributions increased from $349.17 to $463.10, an increase of $113.93, or an increase of 33%. This increase was divided between Congregation Finances and Benevolences as follows.

---

[4]See the section titled "Revised Analysis Factors" in the Introduction for further detail.

Figure 1: **Changes in Per Member Giving in Inflation-Adjusted 1992 Dollars, Total Contributions, Congregational Finances, and Benevolences, 1968-1995**

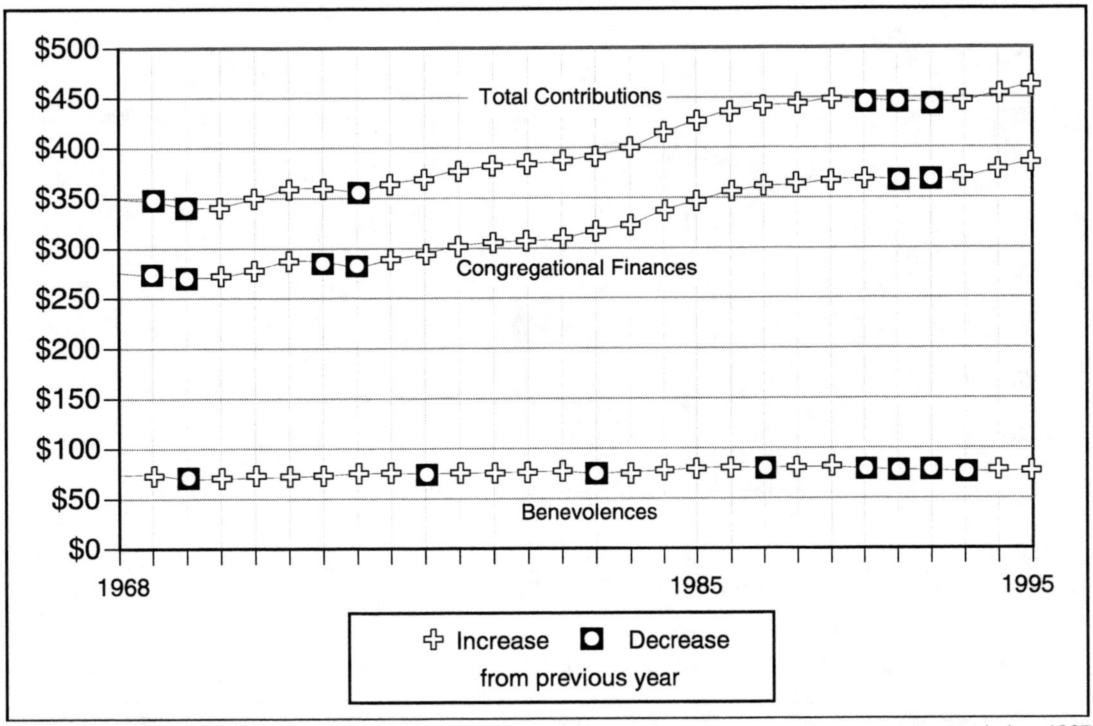

Sources: *Yearbook of American and Canadian Churches,* adjusted series; U.S. Bureau of Economic Analysis

empty tomb, inc. 1997

Congregational Finances increased $110.70, representing a 40% increase.

Benevolences increased $3.23, an increase of 4% per member between 1968 and 1995.

From these allocations, one may observe that while congregations had more to spend to benefit their current members in 1995 compared to 1968, they had only slightly more per member to address Benevolences concerns, which would include the support of denominational offices and seminaries as well as mission activities, both overseas and local.

Figure 2 provides a comparison of per member giving to the categories of Congregational Finances and Benevolences with changes in U.S. per capita disposable personal income in inflation-adjusted 1992 dollars.

Giving as a Percent of Income. The second approach to considering per member giving to churches is the portion of income donated to the church. Individuals choose to spend their incomes to support their lifestyles in a variety of ways; and those incomes have changed over the years, apart from how inflation has affected the dollar. The real growth in the economy is reflected in the fact that U.S. per capita income increased by 68% between 1968 and 1995, after taxes and inflation have been factored out.

U.S. per capita income, an average income figure for the U.S., serves as an average income figure for the broad spectrum of church members included in the composite of 29 denominations. The percentage of U.S. per capita income which church members donated to their congregations provides a measure of what portion of their available resources church

Figure 2: **Per Member Giving to Congregational Finances and Benevolences, and U.S. Per Capita Personal Income, 1968-1995, Inflation-Adjusted 1992 Dollars**

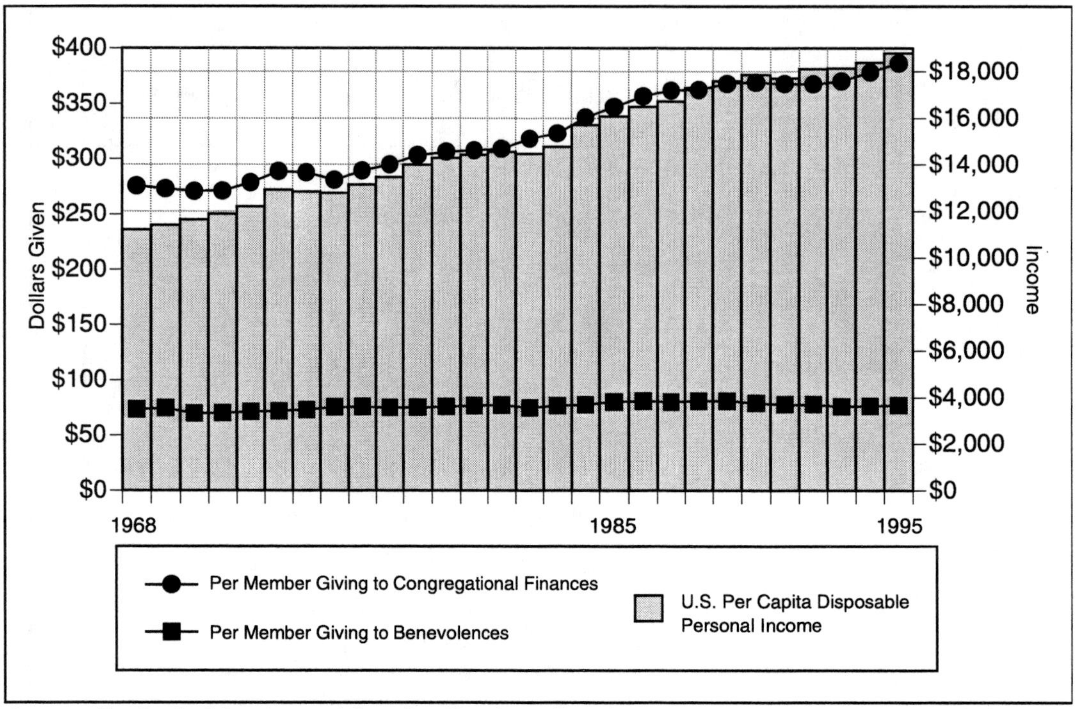

Sources: *Yearbook of American and Canadian Churches,* adjusted series; U.S. Bureau of Economic Analysis

empty tomb, inc. 1997

members directed to religion, as represented by these church structures, from 1968 to 1995. Thus, giving as a percentage of income is one indicator of how religion in America fares in comparison to other lifestyle choices being made by church members.

In Table 2, giving as a percentage of income is presented for per member Total Contributions, and the related subcategories of Congregational Finances and Benevolences. As in Table 1 the arrows by each category indicate whether the percentage of income in that category increased or decreased from the previous year. Inasmuch as the percent figures are rounded to the second decimal place, the arrows indicate the direction of a slight increase or decrease also for those situations in which the percentage provided appears as the same numerical figure as the previous year.

While Table 1 presents data in both current and inflation-adjusted dollars, Table 2 lists a single set of data for giving as a percentage of income. There is no distinction between current or inflation-adjusted dollars when one is considering giving as a percentage of income. The same procedures are applied to both the giving and income dollar amounts when converting current dollars into inflation-adjusted dollars. As long as one compares current dollar giving to current dollar per capita income when calculating the percentage of income, and inflation-adjusted dollar giving to inflation-adjusted dollar per capita income while using the same deflator, the percentages of income will be the same.

A review of Table 2 yields the following information.

Overall, per member giving as a percentage of income to Total Contributions decreased from 3.11% to 2.46%, a decline of 21%. During this same period, U.S. per capita

Table 2:   Per Member Giving as a Percentage of Income, 1968-1995

	Per Full or Confirmed Member Giving to Congregations as a Percentage of Income					
Year	Total Contributions Per Member	↑↓	Congregational Finances	↑↓	Benevolences	↑↓
1968	3.11%		2.46%		0.66%	
1969	3.05%	↓	2.39%	↓	0.65%	↓
1970	2.92%	↓	2.33%	↓	0.60%	↓
1971	2.87%	↓	2.28%	↓	0.59%	↓
1972	2.86%	↓	2.28%	↓	0.58%	↓
1973	2.79%	↓	2.23%	↓	0.56%	↓
1974	2.81%	↑	2.24%	↑	0.57%	↑
1975	2.79%	↓	2.20%	↓	0.59%	↑
1976	2.78%	↓	2.20%	↑	0.58%	↓
1977	2.75%	↓	2.19%	↓	0.56%	↓
1978	2.70%	↓	2.17%	↓	0.54%	↓
1979	2.68%	↓	2.14%	↓	0.53%	↓
1980	2.67%	↓	2.13%	↓	0.53%	↑
1981	2.66%	↓	2.12%	↓	0.53%	↓
1982	2.72%	↑	2.20%	↑	0.52%	↓
1983	2.71%	↓	2.19%	↓	0.52%	↑
1984	2.64%	↓	2.15%	↓	0.49%	↓
1985	2.66%	↑	2.16%	↑	0.50%	↑
1986	2.66%	↓	2.16%	↑	0.49%	↓
1987	2.64%	↓	2.16%	↑	0.48%	↓
1988	2.56%	↓	2.09%	↓	0.47%	↓
1989	2.55%	↓	2.09%	↓	0.46%	↓
1990	2.51%	↓	2.07%	↓	0.44%	↓
1991	2.52%	↑	2.08%	↑	0.44%	↓
1992	2.46%	↓	2.03%	↓	0.43%	↓
1993	2.46%	↑	2.04%	↑	0.42%	↓
1994	2.47%	↑	2.06%	↑	0.42%	↓
1995	2.46%	↓	2.06%	↓	0.41%	↓

Details in the above table may not compute to the numbers shown due to rounding.

income increased 68%, after taxes and inflation. Looking only at current-dollar contributions, one might conclude that church member giving increased at a satisfactory rate. When that money was spent in support of church activities, however, the effects of inflation would become obvious. Thus, the importance of considering inflation-adjusted dollars is underscored.

Yet, another important factor would be missed if only per member giving in inflation-adjusted dollars were considered. While church members increased the amount of dollars they donated to the church between 1968-1995, the increase in the number of dollars donated was not at a rate comparable to the rate of increase in U.S. per capita income. Therefore, those donated dollars represented a smaller portion of the total resources available to church members. In this light, the smaller portion of income being donated to the church in 1995 compared to 1968 suggests that the church was losing market share in the spending patterns of its members.

Out of the 27 two-year periods, giving as a percentage of income for Total Contributions Per Member decreased 21 times from the previous year between 1968 and 1995. The period 1975 to 1981 saw per member giving as a percentage of income decline seven years in a row. There were also two five-year periods of decline, from 1969 to 1973, and from 1986 to 1990.

Congregational Finances decreased 18 times during the same 27 two-year sets in the 1968-1995 period. There were two five-year periods of decline, from 1969 to 1973, and from 1977 to 1981. There was also a three-year period when declines were posted from 1988 to 1990. Congregational Finances declined from 2.46% in 1968 to 2.06% in 1995, a decline of 16%.

Benevolences declined from 0.66% of income in 1968 to 0.41% in 1995, a decline of 38% in the portion of income that was directed to Benevolences. Out of the 27 two-year sets in the 1968-1995 period, the portion of income that went to Benevolences declined 22 times. Although there was a five-year period from 1969 to 1973, the longest period of decline was a ten-year period from 1986 to 1995.

Figure 3 presents per member giving as a percentage of income to Congregational Finances and Benevolences, compared to U.S. per capita income.

Figure 3: **Per Member Giving as a Percentage of Income to Congregational Finances and Benevolences, and U.S. Per Capita Disposable Personal Income, 1968-1995**

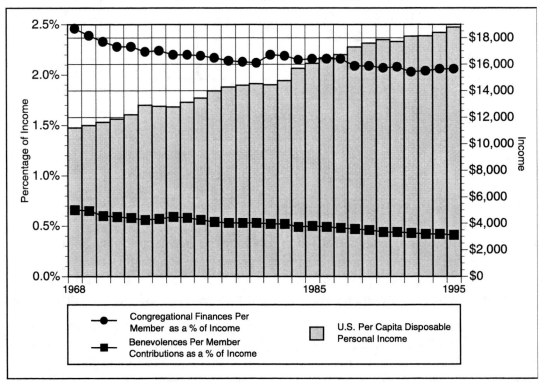

Sources: *Yearbook of American and Canadian Churches,* adjusted series; U.S. Bureau of Economic Analysis

empty tomb, inc. 1997

Giving in Constant Dollars, 1968, 1985 and 1995. The initial report in this series on church member giving considered data for the denominations in the composite for the years 1968 and 1985. With the data now available through 1995, a broader trend can be reviewed for the period under discussion, the 28-year range from 1968 to 1995.

The amount donated to Total Contributions Per Member in inflation-adjusted 1992 dollars was $78.00 greater in 1985 than it was in 1968 for the denominations included in the data set, an average increase of $4.59 a year in per member contributions. There was an overall increase during the 1985-1995 ten-year interval as well. In 1995, the per member contribution to the 29 denominations, which represented 99.95% of the total 1985 membership of the denominations originally studied, was $35.93 more per member in inflation-adjusted dollars than in 1985. The average annual increase was $3.59 between 1985 and 1995, compared to an average annual increase between 1968 and 1985 of $4.59.

Gifts to Congregational Finances also increased between 1968 and 1985, as well as from 1985 to 1995. However, as in the case of Total Contributions, the annual rate of increase declined. Per member contributions to Congregational Finances were $275.54 in 1968, in inflation-adjusted 1992 dollars, and had increased to $346.89 in 1985, a total increase of $71.35, with an average rate of change of $4.20. From 1985 to 1995, the average annual rate of change declined to $3.94, with per member gifts growing from $346.89 in 1985 to $386.24 in 1995, an increase of $39.36.

Benevolences experienced a reversal in the rate of change during the 1985 to 1995 period. In inflation-adjusted 1992 dollars, gifts to Benevolences were $73.63 in 1968 and grew to $80.28 in 1985, an increase of $6.65, with an annual average rate of change of $0.39. Between 1985 and 1995, per member gifts to Benevolences declined to $76.86 in 1995 from the 1985 level of $80.28, a decrease of $3.42, with an annual average rate of change of -$0.34 for the 1985-1995 period.

Table 3 presents per member gifts to Total Contributions, Congregational Finances and Benevolences in inflation-adjusted 1992 dollars for the years 1968, 1985 and 1995.

Table 3: Total Contributions, Congregational Finances and Benevolences, Per Member Giving in Inflation-Adjusted 1992 Dollars, 1968, 1985 and 1995

	Per Member Giving in Inflation-Adjusted 1992 Dollars								
	Total Contributions			Congregational Finances			Benevolences		
Year	Per Member Giving in Adjusted '92 Dollars	Diff. from Previous $ Base	Average Annual Diff. in $s Given	Per Member Giving in Adjusted '92 Dollars	Diff. from Previous $ Base	Average Annual Diff. in $s Given	Per Member Giving in Adjusted '92 Dollars	Diff. from Previous $ Base	Average Annual Diff. in $s Given
1968	$349.17			$275.54			$73.63		
1985	$427.17	$78.00	$4.59	$346.89	$71.35	$4.20	$80.28	$6.65	$0.39
1995	$463.10	$35.93	$3.59	$386.24	$39.36	$3.94	$76.86	-$3.42	-$0.34

Details in the above table may not compute to the numbers shown due to rounding.

Giving as a Percentage of Income, 1968, 1985 and 1995. As noted earlier, per member giving increased $113.93 between 1968 and 1995, an increase of 33% from the 1968 base in inflation-adjusted 1992 dollars. Also noted earlier, during the same 28-year period,

U.S. per capita disposable personal income increased 68% in inflation-adjusted 1992 dollars, from $11,211 in 1968 to $18,790 in 1995.

The difference in the rate of increase between dollars contributed and per capita income explains how church member contributions could be increasing in inflation-adjusted dollars in most of the years from 1968 to 1995, and yet decreasing as a percentage of income in most of the years from 1968 to 1995.

Between 1968 and 1985, Total Contributions declined from 3.11% to 2.66% as a portion of income. The percentage change in giving as a percentage of income from the 1968 base was -14.67% in the 17 years from 1968 to 1985.

From 1985 to 1995, giving as a percentage of income to Total Contributions changed from 2.66% in 1985 to 2.46% in 1995. The percentage change in giving as a percentage of income was -6.19% in this ten-year interval. Therefore, the annual percent change in the portion of per capita income donated to Total Contributions was -0.62% in the 1985-1995 period, compared to the rate of -0.86% in the 1968-1985 period. This data suggests that the rate of annual decline in giving as a percentage of income decreased in the last ten years of the 1968 to 1995 period.

Table 4 presents data for Total Contributions Per member as a percentage of income in summary fashion for the years 1968, 1985 and 1995.

Table 4:   **Per Member Giving as a Percentage of Income to Total Contributions, 1968, 1985 and 1995[5]**

Total Contributions Per Member as a Percentage of Income				
Year	Total Contributions Per Member as a Percentage of Income	Difference in Total Contributions Per Member as a Percentage of Income from Previous Base	Percent Change in Total Contributions Per Member as % of Income Calculated from 1968 Base	Annual Average Percent Change in Total Contributions Per Member as a Percentage of Income
1968	3.11%			
1985	2.66%	-0.46%	-14.67% from 1968	-0.86%
1995	2.46%	-0.19%	-6.19% from 1985	-0.62%

Details in the above table may not compute to the numbers shown due to rounding.

Per member gifts to Congregational Finances measured 2.46% of income in 1968, 2.16% in 1985 and 2.06% in 1995. The annual average percent change in giving as a percentage of income changed from -0.72% a year between 1968 and 1985, from the 1968 base, to -0.42% a year between 1985 and 1995. Once again, the data indicates a decline in the annual decrease in giving as a percentage of income to Congregational Finances in the last ten years of the 1968-1995 period. Table 5 presents this data.

The annual average percent change in giving as a percentage of income to Benevolences held fairly steady between 1985 and 1995, compared to the 1968-1985 period. From 1968

---

[5]See the explanation in the Introduction as to how the 1968-1985 and 1985-1995 rates of change were calculated.

Table 5: **Per Member Giving as a Percentage of Income to Congregational Finances, 1968, 1985 and 1995**

Congregational Finances Per Member as a Percentage of Income				
Year	Cong. Finances Per Member as a Percentage of Income	Difference in Cong. Finances Per Member as a Percentage of Income from Previous Base	Percent Change in Cong. Finances Per Member as % of Income Calculated from 1968 Base	Annual Average Percent Change in Cong. Finances Per Member as a Percentage of Income
1968	2.46%			
1985	2.16%	-0.30%	-12.19% from 1968	-0.72%
1995	2.06%	-0.10%	-4.17% from 1985	-0.42%

Details in the above table may not compute to the numbers shown due to rounding.

to 1985, the portion of member income directed to Benevolences decreased from 0.66% to 0.50%, a decline of -0.16%. This translated to a percent change in giving as a percentage of income of -23.95% from the 1968 base, with an annual average percent change of -1.41%. In the ten-year interval from 1985 to 1995, the percent change in giving as a percentage of income was more than half of the 17-year interval percent change from 1968-1985. Giving as a percentage of income directed to Benevolences declined from 0.50% to 0.41% between 1985 and 1995, a drop of 0.09% during that ten years, compared to a decline of 0.16% in the 17-year interval of 1968-1985. The 1985-1995 percent change in giving as a percentage of income of -13.77% produced an annual average percent change of -1.38%, indicating a very slight improvement from the 1968-1985 seventeen-year rate of -1.41%. Table 6 presents the data for Benevolences as a percentage of income in 1968, 1985 and 1995.

Table 6: **Per Member Giving as a Percentage of Income to Benevolences, 1968, 1985 and 1995**

Benevolences Per Member as a Percentage of Income				
Year	Benevolences Per Member as a Percentage of Income	Difference in Benevolences Per Member as a Percentage of Income from Previous Base	Percent Change in Benevolences Per Member as % of Income Calculated from 1968 Base	Annual Average Percent Change in Benevolences Per Member as a Percentage of Income
1968	0.66%			
1985	0.50%	-0.16%	-23.95% from 1968	-1.41%
1995	0.41%	-0.09%	-13.77% from 1985	-1.38%

Details in the above table may not compute to the numbers shown due to rounding.

Giving in 1994 Compared to 1995. Per member giving as a percentage of income to Total Contributions in 1994 measured 2.47%. In 1995, the figure was 2.46%.

Congregational Finances also declined slightly from 1994 to 1995. Although the level of giving rounded to 2.06% in both 1994 and 1995, there was a decline of -0.42% when the unrounded figures were analyzed.

From 1994 to 1995, Benevolences extended a multiyear pattern of decline, changing from 0.42% in 1994 to 0.41% in 1995, a decline of 1.38% from the 1994 base.

Potential Giving. Apart from the question of whether church members could have been giving a higher percentage of their incomes in 1995 than in 1968, what would have been the situation in 1995 if giving had at least maintained the 1968 percentages of income donated? Rather than the actual 1995 levels of giving, what if giving as a percentage of income in 1995 measured 3.11% for Total Contributions, 2.46% for Congregational Finances, and 0.66% for Benevolences, which were the levels of giving for these three categories in 1968?

Had that been true, per member giving to Total Contributions in current 1995 dollars would have been $629.69 instead of $498.20; Congregational Finances would have been $496.96 instead of $415.52; and Benevolences would have been $132.73 instead of $82.68.

The implications of these differences become clearer when the aggregate totals are calculated by multiplying the theoretical per member giving levels by the number of members reported by these denominations in 1995. Aggregate Total Contributions would then have been $18.8 billion rather than $14.8 billion, a difference of $3.9 billion, or an increase of 26%. Aggregate Congregational Finances would have been $14.8 billion rather than $12.4 billion, a difference of $2.4 billion, or an increase of 20%. There would have been a 61% increase in the total amount received for Benevolences. Instead of receiving $2.5 billion in 1995, as these denominations did, they would have received $4.0 billion, a difference of $1.5 billion.

Summary. Church member giving can be considered on a dollar basis or as a portion of income. The dollar figures indicate how much the receiving church has to spend. The category of percentage of income indicates what portion of total available resources the church member is directing to the church.

While per member contributions to Total Contributions and Congregational Finances increased each year between 1968 and 1995 when considered in current dollars, current dollar per member giving to Benevolences increased in all but one year in the same period.

When inflation was factored out, the data indicated that overall per member giving to all three categories increased, albeit most of the increase in giving was directed to Congregational Finances, with 1995 per member gifts to Benevolences increasing only 4% over the 1968 level.

When considered as a percentage of income, per member gifts to Total Contributions, as well as the two subcategories of Congregational Finances and Benevolences, declined between 1968 and 1995.

While evident throughout the 1968-1985 period, the rate of annual decline decreased in the last ten years of the 1968-1995 period for the categories of Total Contributions and Congregational Finances. However, the rate of decline for the category of Benevolences was at a level during 1985-1995 comparable to that of the 1968-1985 period.

The fact that a smaller portion of income was donated to churches in 1995 than in 1968 meant that the 29 denominations posted smaller aggregate receipts than would have been the case if the portion of income donated to the church had been the same in 1995 as in 1968.

2

Church Member Giving for
49 Denominations, 1994 to 1995_____

The 1968-1995 analysis in chapter one considers data for a group of denominations that published their membership and financial information for 1968 and 1985 in the *Yearbook of American and Canadian Churches (YACC)* series. That data was confirmed for the first edition in this series on church giving reports. Further, that initial set of communions has served as the composite base of denominations analyzed for subsequent data years.

An additional twenty denominations published data for both 1994 and 1995 in the relevant editions of the *YACC* series. By adding the data for these 20 denominations to that of the composite group for these two years, giving patterns in an expanded set of communions can be considered.

In this enlarged comparison, the member sample increased from approximately 30 million to 41 million Full or Confirmed Members, and the number of denominations increased from 29 to 49. The larger group of denominations included both The United Methodist Church and The Episcopal Church, which were not included in the original 1968-1985 analysis because of the unavailability of confirmed 1968 data.[6] A list of the denominations included in the analysis is contained in Appendix A.

Per Member Giving in Inflation-Adjusted 1992 Dollars. As noted in the first chapter of this report, per member giving to Total Contributions increased from 1994 to 1995 for the composite group of 29 denominations in inflation-adjusted 1992 dollars. Specifically, Total Contributions Per Member increased by $8.36 in inflation-adjusted 1992 dollars from 1994 to 1995, from $454.74 in 1994 to $463.10 in 1995. When the group was expanded to 49 denominations, Total Per Member giving increased by $9.97 from 1994 to 1995, from $465.84 in 1994 to $475.81 in 1995.

The composite group of 29 denominations increased per member giving in inflation-adjusted dollars to Congregational Finances by $7.94, from $378.30 in 1994 to $386.24 in 1995. The expanded group increased by $9.63, from $384.34 in 1994 to $393.97 in 1995.

In both groups, giving to Benevolences also increased. In the composite of 29 communions, per member contributions to Benevolences increased from $76.44 to $76.86,

---

[6]The denominational giving data considered in this analysis was obtained from the *Yearbook of American and Canadian Churches*, except as noted in the appendices.

an increase of $0.41 (rounded). There was also an increase in the expanded group of 49 denominations, from $81.49 to $81.84, an increase of $0.35.

It may be noted that although the per member giving increase to Total Contributions in inflation-adjusted 1992 dollars was larger in the expanded group of 49 denominations than it was in the composite of 29 denominations, the increase to Benevolences was smaller in the expanded group of 49 than in the composite of 29 communions.

Table 7 presents the 1994 to 1995 data for the 49 denominations. It also presents the information considered in the following two sections of this chapter.

Table 7:   **Per Member Giving in 49 Denominations, 1994 and 1995, in Inflation-Adjusted 1992 Dollars and as a Percentage of Income**

Year	Full or Confirmed Membership	Total Contributions Per Member		Congregational Finances		Benevolences	
		$s Given in Inflation - Adj. '92 $	Giving as % of Income	$s Given in Inflation - Adj. '92 $	Giving as % of Income	$s Given in Inflation - Adj. '92 $	Giving as % of Income
1994	40,731,011	$465.84	2.53%	$384.34	2.09%	$81.49	0.44%
1995	40,725,705	$475.81	2.53%	$393.97	2.10%	$81.84	0.44%
Difference from the 1994 Base	- 5,306	$9.97	0.00%	$9.63	0.01%	$0.35	0.00%
% Change in Giving as % of Income from the 1994 Base			-0.03%		0.32%		-1.71%

Details in the above table may not compute to the numbers shown due to rounding.

Per Member Giving as a Percentage of Income. In the 1968-1995 composite of 29 denominations, giving as a percentage of income declined to Total Contributions, Congregational Finances and Benevolences from 1994 to 1995. In the composite group of 29 denominations, the percent given to Total Contributions measured a decline from 2.47% in 1994 to 2.46% in 1995. Congregational Finances decreased slightly, although the rounded figures measured 2.06% in 1994 and 2.06% in 1995. Benevolences changed from 0.42% in 1994 to 0.41% in 1995.

In the expanded group of 49 denominations, giving as a percentage of income also decreased to Total Contributions and Benevolences. In this expanded set, the percent of income given on a per member basis to both Total Contributions and Benevolences declined in the unrounded numbers, although the levels reported in Table 7 were the same at the second decimal place in 1994 and 1995. That is, per member giving as a percentage of income to Total Contributions measured 2.53% in 1994 as well as in 1995, and Benevolences measured 0.44% in both 1994 and 1995.

Per member giving as a percentage of income to Congregational Finances increased from 1994 to 1995, changing from 2.09% to 2.10%.

The rate of percent change in giving as a percentage of income for the composite group of 29 denominations was -0.33% from the 1994 base for Total Contributions, compared to -0.03% for the expanded group of 49 denominations. For Congregational

Finances, the composite group of 29 denominations had a rate of -0.07% percent change in giving as a percentage of income from the 1994 base, compared to 0.32% for the expanded group of 49 denominations. Benevolences for the composite group of 29 denominations had a -1.60% percent change in giving as a percentage of income from the 1994 base, compared to a rate of -1.71% for the expanded group of 49 denominations.

Membership, 1994-1995. The Full or Confirmed Membership in the expanded group of 49 denominations decreased from 1994 to 1995. In 1994, these 49 communions reported 40,731,011 members. In 1995, these same denominations reported 40,725,705 members, a decrease of 5,306. This compares with a membership change in the 29 composite denominations from 29,765,898 in 1994 to 29,791,782, an increase of 25,884.

Table 7 presents membership, as well as per member giving data for 1994 and 1995 for the expanded group of 49 denominations in inflation-adjusted 1992 dollars, and as a percentage of income. In addition, the change from 1994 to 1995 in membership, in per member contributions in inflation-adjusted 1992 dollars, in giving as a percentage of income, and in the percent change in giving as a percentage of income from the 1994 base are also presented in the table.

Summary. When the data set of 29 denominations was expanded to include an additional 20 denominations, bringing the total to 49, approximately eleven million additional Full or Confirmed Members were added to the data set. In both the composite of 29 denominations and the expanded group of 49 denominations, per member giving in inflation-adjusted 1992 dollars increased to Total Contributions, Congregational Finances and Benevolences from 1994-1995. However, the increase in per member contributions to Benevolences was smaller in the expanded group of 49 denominations than in the composite group of 29 communions.

Giving as a percentage of income decreased to Total Contributions, Congregational Finances, and Benevolences for the composite group of 29 denominations. In the expanded group, there was a decline in giving as a percentage of income to Total Contributions and Benevolences, and an increase in Congregational Finances.

3

Church Member Giving in Denominations Defined by Organizational Affiliation_____

The 1968-1995 data analysis for the composite of 29 denominations shows that church giving as a percentage of income declined between the years 1968 and 1995. The area of Benevolences showed the largest proportional decrease.

In order to observe whether this trend is common across the theological spectrum, or limited to only certain traditions, two subsets of denominations in the composite group of 29 communions can be identified. These groupings may provide insight into a long-standing assumption, that church members who might be termed "evangelical" give more money to their churches than do church members who belong to what are often termed mainline Protestant denominations.

In the composite group of 29 denominations, eight communions for which financial data is available for 1968, 1985 and 1995 were affiliated with the National Association of Evangelicals (NAE). Eight denominations affiliated with the National Council of the Churches of Christ in the U.S.A. (NCC) also had financial data available for 1968, 1985 and 1995.

Of course, there is diversity of opinion within any denomination, as well as in multi-communion groupings such as the NAE or the NCC. For purposes of the present analysis, however, these two groups may serve as general categories, since they have been characterized as representing certain types of denominations. For example, the National Association of Evangelicals has, by choice of its title, defined its denominational constituency. And traditionally, the National Council of the Churches of Christ in the U.S.A. has counted mainline denominations among its members.

Recognizing that there are limitations in defining a denomination's theological perspectives merely by membership in one of these two organizations, a review of giving patterns of the two subsets of denominations, totaling 16 communions within the larger composite of 29 denominations, may nevertheless provide some insight into how widely spread declining giving patterns may be. Therefore, an analysis of 1968-1995 giving patterns was completed for the two subsets of those denominations which were affiliated with one of these two interdenominational organizations.

Using 1985 data, the eight denominations affiliated with the NAE as of 1995 represented 18% of the total number of NAE-member denominations as listed in the

Yearbook of *American and Canadian Churches* (*YACC*) series; 21% of the total number of NAE-member denominations with membership data listed in the *YACC*; and approximately 21% of the total membership of the NAE-member denominations with membership data listed in the *YACC*.[7]

Data was also available for eight NCC-member denominations in the larger composite group of 29 denominations. Originally, ten of the denominations studied for 1968-1985 were members of the NCC. Two of these denominations merged in 1987, bringing the number of NCC-affiliated denominations in the larger composite to nine communions. Tellingly, another denomination in this original grouping no longer has the staff to compile national data, and therefore is not included in the analysis through 1995, bringing to eight the number of NCC-member denominations in the composite of 29 which had available data for 1968-1995. In 1985, these eight denominations represented 27% of the total number of NCC constituent bodies as listed in the YACC; 30% of the NCC constituent bodies with membership data listed in the YACC; and approximately 29% of the total membership of the NCC constituent bodies with membership data listed in the *YACC*.[8]

Per Member Giving to Total Contributions, 1968, 1985 and 1995. As noted in Table 8, per member giving as a percentage of income to Total Contributions for a composite of those eight NAE-member denominations was 6.14% in 1968. In 1968, per member giving as a percentage of income to Total Contributions was 3.32% for a composite of these eight NCC denominations.

Table 8: Per Member Giving as a Percentage of Income to Total Contributions, for Eight NAE and Eight NCC Denominations, 1968, 1985 and 1995

Total Contributions											
	NAE Denominations					NCC Denominations					
Year	Number of Denom. Analyzed	Total Contrib. Per Member as % of Income	Diff. in Total Contrib. Per Member as % of Income from Previous Base	Percent Change in Total Contrib. as % of Income Figured from 1968 Base	Avg. Annual Percent Change in Total Contrib. as % of Income	Number of Denom. Analyzed	Total Contrib. Per Member as % of Income	Diff. in Total Contrib. Per Member as % of Income from Previous Base	Percent Change in Total Contrib. as % of Income Figured from 1968 Base	Avg. Annual Percent Change in Total Contrib. as % of Income
1968	8	6.14%				8	3.32%			
1985	8	4.84%	-1.30	-21.18% from '68	-1.25%	8	2.92%	-0.40	-12.11% from '68	-0.71%
1995	8	4.08%	-0.76	-12.31% from '85	-1.23%	8	2.90%	-0.02	-0.52% from '85	-0.05%

Details in the above table may not compute to the numbers shown due to rounding.

[7] The 1985 total church membership estimate of 3,388,414 represented by NAE denominations includes *YACC* 1985 membership data for each denomination where available or, if 1985 membership data was not available, membership data for the most recent year prior to 1985. Full or Confirmed membership data was used except in those instances where this figure was not available, in which case Inclusive Membership was used.

[8] The 1985 total church membership estimate of 39,621,950 represented by NCC denominations includes *YACC* 1985 membership data for each denomination where available or, if 1985 membership data was not available, membership data for the most recent year prior to 1985. Full or Confirmed membership data was used except in those instances where this figure was not available, in which case Inclusive Membership was used.

In 1985, the NAE denominations' per member giving as a percentage of income level was 4.84%, while the NCC level was 2.92%.

The data shows the NAE-member denominations received a larger portion of their members' incomes than did NCC-affiliated denominations in both 1968 and 1985. This information supports the assumption that denominations identifying with an evangelical perspective received a higher level of support than denominations that may be termed mainline.

The analysis also presents another finding. The decline in levels of giving observed in the larger composite of 29 denominations was also evident among both the NAE-member denominations and the NCC-member denominations. While giving levels decreased for both sets of denominations between 1968 and 1985, the decrease was more pronounced in the NAE-affiliated communions in Total Contributions. The percent change in percentage of income donated in the NAE-member denominations, in comparison to the 1968 base, declined 21% between 1968 and 1985, while the percent change in percentage of income given to the NCC-member denominations declined 12%.

Thus, although the evangelical church members continued to give more than mainline church members, the difference in giving levels was smaller in 1985 than in 1968.

A decline in giving as a percentage of income continued among the eight NAE-member denominations during the 1985-1995 period. By 1995, per member giving as a percentage of income to Total Contributions had declined from the 1985 level of 4.84% to 4.08%, a percentage drop of 12% in the portion of members' incomes donated over that ten-year interval.

Meanwhile, the eight NCC-affiliated denominations also declined in giving as a percentage of income to Total Contributions during 1985-1995, from the 1985 level of 2.92% to 2.90% in 1995, a percentage decline of 0.52% in the portion of income given to these churches.

Because of the decline in the portion of income given in the NAE-affiliated denominations, in 1995 the difference in per member giving as a percentage of income between the NAE-affiliated denominations and the NCC-affiliated denominations was not as large as it had been in 1968. Comparing the two rates in giving as a percentage of income to Total Contributions between the NAE-member denominations and the NCC-member denominations in this analysis, the NCC-affiliated denominations received 54% as much of per member income as the NAE-member denominations did in 1968, 60% as much in 1985, and 71% in 1995.

For the NAE-affiliated denominations, during the 1985 to 1995 period, the rate of decrease in the average annual percent change in per member giving as a percentage of income to Total Contributions continued at a rate comparable to the 1968-1985 annual percent change from the 1968 base. The 1968-1985 average annual percent change was -1.25%. The figure for 1985-1995 was -1.23%.

In the NCC-member denominations, the trend slowed. While the average annual percent change from the 1968 base in giving as a percentage of income was -0.71% between 1968 and 1985, the average annual change from 1985 was -0.05% between 1985 and 1995.

Per Member Giving to Congregational Finances and Benevolences, 1968, 1985 and 1995. Were there any markedly different patterns between the two subsets of denominations defined by affiliation with the NAE and the NCC in regards to the distribution of Total Contributions between the subcategories of Congregational Finances and Benevolences?

In fact, both subsets of communions displayed the same trend noted in the composite group of 29 denominations. Between 1968 and 1995, both categories of Congregational Finances and Benevolences declined as a percentage of income in the NCC-affiliated denominations as well as in the NAE-affiliated group. It may be noted, however, that the NCC-related denominations showed an increase in the percentage of income donated to Congregational Finances in the 1985 to 1995 period.

Table 9 presents the Congregational Finances giving data for the NAE and NCC denominations in 1968, 1985 and 1995.

Table 9: **Per Member Giving as a Percentage of Income to Congregational Finances in Eight NAE and Eight NCC Denominations, 1968, 1985 and 1995**

	Congregational Finances									
	NAE Denominations					NCC Denominations				
Year	Number of Denom. Analyzed	Cong. Finances Per Member as % of Income	Diff. in Cong. Finances Per Member as % of Income from Previous Base	Percent Change in Cong. Finances as % of Income Figured from 1968 Base	Avg. Annual Percent Change in Cong. Finances as % of Income	Number of Denom. Analyzed	Cong. Finances Per Member as % of Income	Diff. in Cong. Finances Per Member as % of Income from Previous Base	Percent Change in Cong. Finances as % of Income Figured from 1968 Base	Avg. Annual Percent Change in Cong. Finances as % of Income
1968	8	4.99%				8	2.69%			
1985	8	3.90%	-1.09%	-21.92% from '68	-1.29%	8	2.46%	-0.23%	-8.37% from '68	-0.49%
1995	8	3.34%	-0.56%	-11.12% from '85	-1.11%	8	2.53%	0.07%	2.56% from '85	0.26%

Details in the above table may not compute to the numbers shown due to rounding.

Table 10 presents the Benevolences giving data for the NAE and NCC denominations in 1968, 1985 and 1995.

In 1968, the NAE-affiliated members were giving 6.14% of their incomes to their churches. Of that, 4.99% went to Congregational Finances, while 1.15% went to Benevolences. In 1985, of the 4.84% of income donated to Total Contributions, 3.90% was directed to Congregational Finances. This represented a percent change in the portion of income going to Congregational Finances of -22% from the 1968 base. Per member contributions to Benevolences among these NAE-member denominations declined from 1.15% in 1968 to 0.94% in 1985, representing a percent change of -18% from the 1968 base in the portion of income donated to Benevolences.

In 1995, the 4.08% of income donated by the NAE-member denominations to their churches was divided between Congregational Finances and Benevolences at the 3.34% and 0.74% levels, respectively. The percent change between 1985 and 1995 in contributions to Congregational Finances as a percent of income was a decline of 11%. In contrast, the percent

Table 10:   **Per Member Giving as a Percentage of Income to Benevolences in Eight NAE and Eight NCC Denominations, 1968, 1985 and 1995**

	Benevolences										
	NAE Denominations					NCC Denominations					
Year	Number of Denom. Analyzed	Benevol. Per Member as % of Income	Diff. in Benevol. Per Member as % of Income from Previous Base	Percent Change in Benevol. as % of Income Figured from 1968 Base	Avg. Annual Percent Change in Benevol. as % of Income	Number of Denom. Analyzed	Benevol. Per Member as % of Income	Diff. in Benevol. Per Member as % of Income from Previous Base	Percent Change in Benevol. as % of Income Figured from 1968 Base	Avg. Annual Percent Change in Benevol. as % of Income
1968	8	1.15%				8	0.63%			
1985	8	0.94%	-0.21%	-17.98% from '68	-1.06%	8	0.45%	-0.18%	-28.04% from '68	-1.65%
1995	8	0.74%	-0.20%	-17.46% from '85	-1.75%	8	0.37%	-0.08%	-13.62% from '85	-1.36%

Details in the above table may not compute to the numbers shown due to rounding.

change in contributions to Benevolences as a percent of income was a decline of 17% in the same ten-year interval. The annual rate in the percent change in giving as a percentage of income to Benevolences accelerated to -1.75% percent between 1985 and 1995, compared to the 1968-1985 rate of -1.06%.

In 1968, the NCC-member denominations were giving 3.32% of their incomes to their churches. Of that, 2.69% went to Congregational Finances. In 1985, of the 2.92% of income donated to these communions, 2.46% went to Congregational Finances. This represented a percent change from the 1968 base in the portion of income going to Congregational Finances of -8%. In contrast, per member contributions as a percent of income to Benevolences among these same NCC-affiliated denominations had declined from 0.63% in 1968 to 0.45% in 1985, representing a percent change of -28% from the 1968 base in the portion of income donated to Benevolences.

In 1995, the 2.90% of income donated by the NCC-affiliated members to their churches was divided between Congregational Finances and Benevolences at the 2.53% and 0.37% levels, respectively. Although the per member Total Contributions as a percent of income decreased from 2.92% to 2.90% between 1985 and 1995, the amount of income directed to Congregational Finances increased, from 2.46% in 1985 to 2.53% in 1995. The 1995 percent change in contributions to Congregational Finances as a percent of income from 1985 was an increase of 3%.

The portion of income directed to Benevolences by these NCC-member denominations had declined from 1968 to 1985, and continued to decline from 1985 to 1995. The percent change in contributions to Benevolences as a percent of income had declined from 0.45% in 1985 to the 1995 level of 0.37%, a decline of 14% in this ten-year interval. The annual percent change from 1985 in giving as a percentage of income to Benevolences indicated a lower rate of decline at 1.36% between 1985 and 1995, compared to the 1968-1985 annual rate of -1.65%.

Figure 4 presents data for giving as a percentage of income to Total Contributions, Congregational Finances and Benevolences for both the NAE and NCC denominations in graphic form for the years 1968, 1985 and 1995.

Figure 4: **Per Member Giving as a Percentage of Income to Total Contributions, Congregational Finances and Benevolences, Eight NAE and Eight NCC Denominations, 1968, 1985 and 1995**

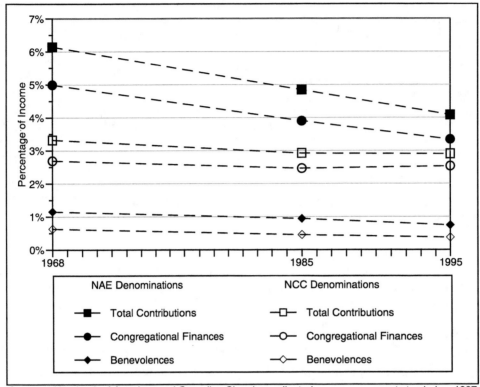

Sources: *Yearbook of American and Canadian Churches,* adjusted series; U.S. Bureau of Economic Analysis   empty tomb, inc. 1997

Changes in Per Member Giving, 1968 to 1995. For the NAE-affiliated denominations, per member giving as a percentage of income to Congregational Finances declined from 4.99% in 1968 to 3.34% in 1995, a change of -33.0% from the 1968 base. In Benevolences, the -35.4% change was due to a decline from 1.15% in 1968 to 0.74% in 1995.

For the NCC-affiliated denominations, between 1968 and 1995, per member giving as a percentage of income declined from 2.69% to 2.53%, a change of -5.8% in the subcategory of Congregational Finances. That compared to the -41.7% decline in the subcategory of Benevolences that changed from 0.63% in 1968 to 0.37% in 1995.

Table 11 presents the 1968-1995 percent change in per member giving as a percentage of income to Total Contributions, Congregational Finances and Benevolences in both the NAE- and NCC-affiliated communions.

Per Member Giving in Inflation-Adjusted 1992 Dollars. The NAE-affiliated group level of per member support to Total Contributions in inflation-adjusted 1992 dollars was $688.09 in 1968. This increased to $777.57 in 1985, and declined by 1995 to $767.04.

For the NAE-affiliated denominations, per member contributions in inflation-adjusted 1992 dollars to the subcategory of Congregational Finances increased from 1968 to 1985, and again from 1985 to 1995. Per member contributions in inflation-adjusted 1992 dollars to Benevolences followed the same pattern as Total Contributions, increasing between 1968 and 1985, and decreasing between 1985 and 1995.

Table 11: **Percent Change in Per Member Giving as a Percentage of Income in Eight NAE and Eight NCC Denominations, 1968 to 1995**

	NAE Denominations				NCC Denominations			
Year	Number of Denom. Analyzed	Total Contrib.	Cong. Finances	Benevol.	Number of Denom. Analyzed	Total Contrib.	Cong. Finances	Benevol.
1968	8	6.14%	4.99%	1.15%	8	3.32%	2.69%	0.63%
1995	8	4.08%	3.34%	0.74%	8	2.90%	2.53%	0.37%
% Chg. 1968-95	8	-33.39%	-33.04%	-35.44%	8	-12.63%	-5.81%	-41.65%

Details in the above table may not compute to the numbers shown due to rounding.

The NCC-affiliated group experienced an increase in constant dollar per member Total Contributions between 1968 and 1995. The 1968 NCC level of per member support in inflation-adjusted 1992 dollars was $372.30. In 1985, this had increased to $469.13, and in 1995 the figure was $545.17.

The NCC-member denominations experienced an increase in constant dollar per member donations to Congregational Finances in both 1985 and 1995 as well. However, while gifts to Benevolences increased between 1968 and 1985 in inflation-adjusted 1992 dollars, the level of per member contributions to Benevolences decreased between 1985 and 1995.

As a portion of Total Contributions, the NAE-member denominations directed 19% of their per member gifts to Benevolences in 1968, 19% in 1985 and 18% in 1995. The NCC-member denominations directed 19% of their per member gifts to Benevolences in 1968, 16% in 1985 and 13% in 1995.

Table 12 below presents the levels of per member giving to Total Contributions, Congregational Finances and Benevolences, in inflation-adjusted 1992 dollars, and the percentage of Total Contributions which went to Benevolences in 1968, 1985 and 1995, for both sets of denominations. In addition, the percent change from the 1968 base in per member inflation-adjusted 1992 dollar contributions from 1968 to 1995 is noted.

Table 12: **Per Member Giving in Eight NAE and Eight NCC Denominations, 1968, 1985 and 1995, Inflation-Adjusted 1992 Dollars.**

	NAE Denominations					NCC Denominations				
Year	Number of Denom. Analyzed	Total Contrib.	Cong. Finances	Benevol.	Benevol. as % of Total Contrib.	Number of Denom. Analyzed	Total Contrib.	Cong. Finances	Benevol.	Benevol. as % of Total Contrib.
1968	8	$688.09	$559.40	$128.69	19%	8	$372.30	$301.48	$70.82	19%
1985	8	$777.57	$626.24	$151.34	19%	8	$469.13	$396.06	$73.07	16%
1995	8	$767.04	$627.79	$139.26	18%	8	$545.17	$475.92	$69.26	13%
$ Diff. '68-'95		$78.95	$68.39	$10.56			$172.87	$174.43	-$1.56	
% Chg. '68-'95		11%	12%	8%			46%	58%	-2%	

Details in the above table may not compute to the numbers shown due to rounding

Figure 5 presents the data for per member contributions in inflation-adjusted 1992 dollars in graphic form for the years 1968, 1985 and 1995.

Figure 5:   Per Member Giving to Total Contributions, Congregational Finances and Benevolences in Eight NAE and Eight NCC Member Denominations, 1968, 1985 and 1995, Inflation-Adjusted 1992 Dollars

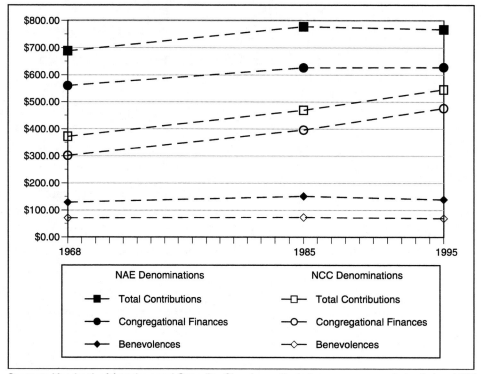

Sources: *Yearbook of American and Canadian Churches,* adjusted series; U.S. Bureau of Economic Analysis   empty tomb, inc. 1997

Aggregate Dollar Donations, 1968 and 1995. A decrease from 1968 to 1995 in per member giving as a percentage of income to all categories among the NAE-member and NCC-member denominations in this analysis suggests that the decline in giving patterns is evident among church members, and the church structures they support, across the theological spectrum. Whatever factors are contributing to this decline, they are not limited to one specific part of the church.

In terms of per member inflation-adjusted 1992 dollar gifts among the NCC-member churches, the data indicates an increase to Total Contributions and Congregational Finances, but a decline in per member gifts to Benevolences. A number of the NCC-affiliated denominations have experienced a decline in income resulting in staff cutbacks at the national, and in some cases regional, levels.

However, while the mainline denominations have conducted highly publicized downsizing during the 1968-1995 period, a similar pattern was not evident among the evangelical communions during these same years. A contributing factor to this difference is the growth in members that the evangelical denominations experienced, in contrast to the membership decline reported by the mainline denominations.

The difference between the two groupings of denominations is that, while both decreased in per member giving to Benevolences as a percentage of income, the NAE-member denominations grew in membership, and the NCC-member denominations declined in membership. In the NAE-affiliated communions, while members were giving a smaller percentage of income to Benevolences in 1995 than in 1968, the aggregate total dollars available increased, as indicated in Table 13 below. For the NCC-affiliated communions, a decline in per member giving as a percentage of income, as well as in inflation-adjusted 1992 dollars to Benevolences, was coupled with a decrease in membership. Thus, for the NCC-affiliated communions, there was a decrease in constant dollars in aggregate Benevolences between 1968 and 1995, as presented in Table 14 below.

Table 13 considers aggregate giving data for the eight NAE-member denominations included in this study for which data was available for both 1968 and 1995. Membership in these eight NAE-member denominations increased 52% from 1968-1995. As noted earlier, although per member giving as a percentage of income declined to Total Contributions and the two subcategories of Congregation Finances and Benevolences for the NAE-affiliated denominations, per member giving in inflation-adjusted dollars increased in each of the three categories from 1968 to 1995.

As measured in current dollars, giving in each of the three categories of Total Contributions, Congregational Finances and Benevolences was greater in 1995 than in 1968 for the NAE-member denominations.

The same can be said for the three aggregate categories when inflation was factored out by converting the current dollars to inflation-adjusted 1992 dollars. These denominations have been compensated for a decline in giving as a percentage of income by the increase in total membership. As long as these denominations continue to grow in membership and maintain constant levels of giving, their programs may not be affected in the immediate future in the same way some of the mainline Protestant communions have been impacted by a combination of declining giving and membership.

Table 13: **Aggregate Giving, Eight NAE Denominations, 1968 and 1995, in Current and Inflation-Adjusted 1992 Dollars**

Year	Number of Den. Analyzed	Member-ship	Current Dollars			Inflation-Adjusted 1992 Dollars		
			Total Contributions	Cong. Finances	Benevol.	Total Contributions	Cong. Finances	Benevol.
1968	8	535,522	$101.923.579	$82,861,129	$19,062,450	$368,487,270	$299,570,242	$68,917,028
1995	8	815,836	$673,213,030	$550,992,076	$122,220,954	$625,778,983	$512,169,619	$113,609,364
% Chg.		52%	560%	565%	541%	70%	71%	65%

Details in the above table may not compute to the numbers shown due to rounding.

Table 14 below considers aggregate data for the eight NCC-member denominations for which both 1968 and 1995 data was available. The NCC-related denominations also experienced an increase in current dollars in each of the three categories of Total Contributions, Congregational Finances and Benevolences, even with a posted decline in membership.

However, the inflation-adjusted 1992 dollar figures account for the acknowledged financial difficulties in many of these communions, particularly in the category of

Benevolences. The decline in membership affected the total income received by this group of denominations. Between 1968 and 1995, while the NCC-related communions experienced an increase of 46% in per member giving to Total Contributions in inflation-adjusted 1992 dollars—from $372.30 in 1968 to $545.17 in 1995—aggregate Total Contributions in 1995 to these eight denominations were only 10% larger in inflation-adjusted 1992 dollars in 1995 than in 1968.

In regard to the two categories of Congregational Finances and Benevolences, Congregational Finances absorbed the increased giving. The -27% decline in aggregated Benevolences receipts in inflation-adjusted 1992 dollars between 1968 and 1995 provides insight into the basis for any cutbacks at the denominational level.

Table 14: **Aggregate Giving, Eight NCC Denominations, 1968 and 1995, in Current and Inflation-Adjusted 1992 Dollars**

Year	Number of Den. Analyzed	Member-ship	Current Dollars			Inflation-Adjusted 1992 Dollars		
			Total Contributions	Cong. Finances	Benevol.	Total Contributions	Cong. Finances	Benevol.
1968	8	12,876,821	$1,326,045,714	$1,073,798,710	$252,247,004	$4,794,091,518	$3,882,135,611	$911,955,907
1995	8	9,658,026	$5,664,421,895	$4,944,828,071	$719,593,824	$5,265,311,299	$4,596,419,475	$668,891,824
% Chg.		-25%	327%	360%	185%	10%	18%	-27%

Details in the above table may not compute to the numbers shown due to rounding.

Summary. An analysis of giving as a percentage of income found a negative trend in church member giving across the theological spectrum between 1968 and 1995. Denominations affiliated with both the NAE and the NCC were receiving a smaller portion of income on a per member basis.

On one hand, the NAE-member denominations received a higher portion of income on a per member basis than did the NCC-member denominations throughout this period. On the other hand, between 1968 and 1985, the NAE-member denominations experienced a higher rate of decrease in average annual percent change in giving as a percentage of income from the 1968 base in the categories of Total Contributions and Congregational Finances than did the NCC-member denominations. In the category of Benevolences, between 1968 and 1985, the NCC-member denominations had a higher rate of decrease in average annual percent change in giving as a percentage of income from the 1968 base than did the NAE-member denominations.

Between 1985 and 1995, the NAE-member denominations experienced a higher rate of decrease in average annual percent change in per member giving as a percentage of income from the 1985 base than did the NCC-member denominations in each of the three categories of Total Contributions, Congregational Finances and Benevolences. Further, in the category of Congregational Finances, the NCC-member denominations increased somewhat from 1985 to 1995.

In the NAE-member denominations, the rate of decrease in per member giving as a percentage of income to Benevolences quickened during the 1985-1995 period compared to the 1968-1985 period. In the NCC-member denominations, the rate of decrease in per member giving as a percentage of income to Benevolences slowed between 1985-1995, compared to 1968-1985.

After inflation was factored out by converting the data to inflation-adjusted 1992 dollars, both the NAE-affiliated and the NCC-affiliated denominations received more dollars per member for the categories of Total Contributions and Congregational Finances in 1995 than in 1968. In the Benevolences category, the NAE-affiliated denominations received $10.56 more per member in inflation-adjusted 1992 dollars, an increase of 8% between 1968 and 1995. The NCC-affiliated denominations received $1.56 less per member in inflation-adjusted 1992 dollars, a decline of 2%.

The NAE-affiliated denominations were growing in membership during the 1968-1995 period. As a result, aggregate income to these denominations also increased. A decline in per member giving in inflation-adjusted 1992 dollars to Benevolences in the NCC-affiliated denominations coincided with a decline in membership in those denominations. The result was a decrease in aggregate Benevolences for the NCC-member denominations between 1968 and 1995.

The generally-held belief that evangelicals were "better givers" than mainline members is correct in that per member giving was higher in the NAE-affiliated denominations both in terms of giving as a percentage of income and constant dollar contributions when compared to NCC-member denominations throughout the 1968 to 1995 period.

However, the rate of decline in per member giving as a percentage of income between 1985 and 1995 was more pronounced among the NAE-affiliated denominations than among the NCC-affiliated denominations.

The negative direction in per member giving as a percentage of income over the 28-year time span under review in both the NAE-affiliated and NCC-affiliated denominations suggests that the negative trend in giving patterns is not limited to a particular portion of the theological spectrum.

4

Church Member Giving in Eleven Denominations, 1921-1995_____

According to the composite data for 29 Protestant denominations, the portion of income given to the church declined over the last 28 years, from 1968-1995.

How do the giving patterns in this 28-year period compare to church member giving data throughout most of this century? Was there a time frame during which giving was increasing, or where giving levels were consistently higher than others?

Unfortunately, comparable data is not readily available for all 29 communions in the composite analysis throughout this century. However, data over an extended period of time is available in the *Yearbook of American and Canadian Churches* series for a group of 11 Protestant communions, or their historical antecedents. These include ten mainline Protestant communions and the Southern Baptist Convention.

The available data has been reported fairly consistently over the time span of 1921 to 1995.[9] The value of the multiyear comparison is that it provides a historical time line over which to observe giving patterns.

Giving as a Percentage of Income. The period under consideration in this section of the report began in 1921. At that point, per member giving as a percentage of income was 2.9%. In current dollars, U.S. per capita disposable (after-tax) personal income was $555, and per member giving was $16. When inflation was factored out by converting both income and giving to 1992 dollars, per capita income in 1921 measured $4,479 and per member giving was $130.

From 1922 through 1933, giving as a percent of income stayed above the 3% level. The high was 3.68% in 1924, followed closely by the amount in 1932, when per member giving measured 3.65% of per capita income. This trend was of interest since per capita

_____

[9]Data for the period 1965-1967 was not available in a form that could be readily analyzed for the present purposes, and therefore data for these three years was estimated by dividing the change in per member current dollar contributions from 1964 to 1968 by four, the number of years in this interval, and cumulatively adding the result to the base year of 1964 data and subsequently to the calculated data for the succeeding years of 1965 and 1966 in order to obtain estimates for the years 1965-1967.

income was increasing steadily between 1921 to 1927. Even as people were increasing in personal affluence, they also continued to maintain a giving level of more than 3% to their churches.

The year 1933 was the depth of the Great Depression. Per capita income was at the lowest point it would reach between 1921 and 1995, whether measured in current or inflation-adjusted dollars. Yet per member giving as a percentage of income was 3.3%. Income had decreased by 17% between 1921 and 1933 in inflation-adjusted 1992 dollars, from $4,479 to $3,727. Meanwhile, per member giving had decreased 6%, from $130 in 1921 to $123 in 1933, in inflation-adjusted dollars. Therefore, giving as a percentage of income actually increased from 2.9% in 1921 to 3.3% in 1933, an increase of 13% in the portion of income contributed to the church.

Giving in inflation-adjusted 1992 dollars declined from 1933 to 1934, and again in 1935, even though income began to recover. In inflation-adjusted dollars, giving did not recover to the 1927 level of $200 until 1953, when giving grew from $192 in 1952 to $211 in 1953.

During World War II, incomes improved rapidly. Meanwhile, church member giving increased only modestly in current dollars. When inflation was factored out, per member giving was at $126.61 in 1941, declined to $123.24 in 1942, increased in 1943 to $124.73, and then to $136.98 in 1944. However, income in inflation-adjusted dollars grew from $6,061 in 1941 to $7,061 in 1942, $7,542 in 1943, and reached a high of $7,949 in 1944, a level that would not be surpassed again until 1953. Thus, giving as a percentage of income reached a low-point of 1.7% during 1942, 1943 and 1944, the three full calendar years of formal U.S. involvement in World War II.

In 1945, the last year of the war, U.S. per capita income was $7,850 in inflation-adjusted dollars. Giving in inflation-adjusted dollars was $155 that year. Although per member giving increased 26% between 1933 and 1945, per capita income had increased 111%. Giving as a percentage of income therefore declined from the 3.3% level in 1933, to 2.0% in 1945.

The unusually high level of per capita income slumped after the war but had recovered to war levels by the early 1950s. By 1960, U.S. per capita income was 10% higher in inflation-adjusted 1992 dollars than it had been in 1945, increasing from $7,850 in 1945 to $8,647 in 1960. Meanwhile, per member giving in inflation-adjusted dollars had increased 75%, from $155 in 1945 to $272 in 1960. Accordingly, giving as a percentage of income reached a postwar high of 3.15% in 1960.

By 1968, giving as a percentage of income had declined to 2.7% for this group of 11 communions. U.S. per capita income increased 30% in inflation-adjusted 1992 dollars between 1960 and 1968, from $8,647 in 1960 to $11,211 in 1968. However, per member giving had only increased 10% in inflation-adjusted dollars, from the 1960 level of $272 to the 1968 level of $298.

By 1985, per member giving had increased 32% in inflation-adjusted 1992 dollars, from $298 in 1968 to $393 in 1985. U.S. per capita income measured $16,074, an increase of 43% over the 1968 level of $11,211. Giving as a percentage of income measured 2.45% in 1985.

The year 1995 was the latest year for which data was available for the eleven denominations considered in this section. In that year, per member giving as a percentage of income was 2.39%, a slight decline from the 1985 level of 2.45%. Per member giving had increased 14% in inflation-adjusted 1992 dollars, from $393 in 1985 to $449 in 1995. However, U.S. per capita income had increased 17% during this period, from the 1985 level of $16,074 to the 1995 level of $18,790.

Figure 6 contrasts per member giving as a percentage of income for a composite of eleven Protestant denominations, with U.S. disposable personal income in inflation-adjusted 1992 dollars, for the period 1921 through 1995.

Figure 6:   Per Member Giving as a Percentage of Income in 11 Denominations, and U.S. Per Capita Income 1921-1995

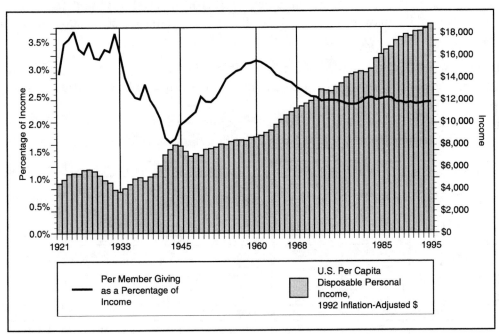

Sources: *Yearbook of American and Canadian Churches,* adjusted series; U.S. Bureau of Economic Analysis   empty tomb, inc. 1997

Change in Per Member Giving and U.S. Per Capita Disposable Personal Income, in Inflation-adjusted 1992 Dollars. For this group of 11 communions, per member giving in inflation-adjusted 1992 dollars increased in the majority of years during the 1921-1947 period. Per member giving in inflation-adjusted dollars decreased from 1924 to 1925. While it increased from 1925 to 1926 and again in 1927, giving began a seven-year decline in 1928. This seven-year period, from 1928 to 1934, included the worst years of the Great Depression. Giving increased again in 1935. Declines in 1939, 1940, 1942, 1946 and 1947 alternated with increases in the other years.

Then, from 1947 through 1968,[10] these 11 communions experienced uninterrupted increases in per member giving in inflation-adjusted 1992 dollars for 21 years in a row.

---

[10] Excluding the years 1965 through 1967 for which estimated data is used. See first footnote in this chapter.

Further, the period from 1947 to the year 1960, when giving as a percentage of income reached its postwar peak, posted the highest prolonged annual increase in per member giving in inflation-adjusted dollars during this 1921-1995 75-year period. During the 1947-1960 13-year interval, per member giving averaged an increase of $9.57 a year. Although giving continued to increase for the next few years from 1960 to 1968, it was at the much slower rate of $3.26 per year.

Per member giving in inflation-adjusted dollars declined annually from 1968 through 1971, followed by two years of increase and two of decline.

The next highest period of sustained increased was the 20-year interval of 1975-1995. During this period, income increased an average of $300.33 annually in inflation-adjusted 1992 dollars. Meanwhile, per member giving increased $6.99 on average each year, a rate slightly less than the 1947-1968 annual increase of $7.16. Overall, giving increased 45% from 1975 to 1995, while income increased 47%. Therefore, giving as a percentage of income was 2.42% in 1975 and 2.39% in 1995.

By reviewing this data in five-year periods from 1950 to 1995, as presented in Table 15, the time period in which giving began to decline markedly can be identified.

Table 15: Average Annual Increase in U.S. Per Capita Income and Per Member Giving in 11 Denominations, 1950-1995, Inflation-adjusted 1992 Dollars

Time Period	U.S. Per Capita Income			Per Member Giving			Avg. Ann. Chg. Giv. as % Avg. Ann. Chg. Income
	First Year in Period	Last Year in Period	Average Annual Change	First Year in Period	Last Year in Period	Average Annual Change	
1950-1955	$7,556	$8,241	$136.98	$181.36	$237.61	$11.25	8.21%
1955-1960	$8,241	$8,647	$81.19	$237.61	$272.14	$6.91	8.51%
1960-1964[11]	$8,647	$9,755	$277.02	$272.14	$281.30	$2.29	0.83%
1964-1970[11]	$9,755	$11,639	$314.06	$281.00	$296.61	$2.55	0.81%
1970-1975	$11,639	$12,783	$228.77	$296.61	$309.32	$2.54	1.11%
1975-1980	$12,783	$14,409	$325.07	$309.32	$337.96	$5.73	1.76%
1980-1985	$14,409	$16,074	$333.00	$337.96	$393.31	$11.07	3.32%
1985-1990	$16,074	$17,859	$357.01	$393.31	$422.13	$5.76	1.61%
1990-1995	$17,859	$18,790	$232.79	$422.13	$449.06	$6.73	2.89%

Details in the above table may not compute to the numbers shown due to rounding.

As indicated in Table 15, the period 1950 to 1955 was the period of highest annual increase in per member giving in inflation-adjusted 1992 dollars. The period 1955 to 1960 was the period of highest annual increase in giving as a percentage of the annual change in U.S. per capita income. The period 1980 to 1985 produced a higher average per member annual dollar increase than that given in 1955-1960. However, the larger amount of $11.07 represented only 3.32% of the average annual increase in U.S. per capita income, compared to the 8.51% which the $6.91 increase in giving represented from 1955 to 1960.

Giving declined markedly between 1960 and 1964 in these communions.[11] While income was increasing at an annual rate of $277 in this four-year period, 241% greater than

---

[11] See the first footnote in this chapter for an explanation of the selection of 1960-1964 and 1964-1970, rather than 1960-1965 and 1965-1970.

in the 1955-1960 period, the average annual increase in per member contributions in inflation-adjusted 1992 dollars was $2.29, 67% smaller in 1960-1964 than it was in 1955-1960.

The 1960-1964 period predates many of the controversial issues often cited as reasons for declining giving. Also, it was at the end of the 1960-1964 period when membership began to decrease in mainline denominations, ten of which are included in this group. Therefore, additional exploration of that period of time might be merited.

Increases in per member giving were consistently low from 1960-1975. The annual rate of increase was $2.29 per year from 1960 to 1964, $2.55 from 1964 to 1970, and $2.54 from 1970 to 1975. Throughout the 1960 to 1970 period, the increase in dollars given represented less than one percent of the average annual increase in per capita income, while from 1970-1975, it was 1.11%.

In the 1975-1980 period, the average annual increase in giving increased to $5.73, representing 1.76% of the average annual increase in per capita income.

From 1980 to 1985, the average annual increase in giving rose to $11.07. This amount of $11.07—representing 3.32% of the average annual increase in income during the 1980-1985 period—was the second highest average annual rate of increase in terms of per member giving in inflation-adjusted dollars during the 1950 to 1995 period. As a portion of the increase in per capita income, the 3.32% of the 1980 to 1985 period was the third largest annual rate of increase in the 1950 to 1995 period.

The annual average increase in giving as a percent of the average annual income increase from 1985 to 1990 fell below that of both the 1975 to 1980 and 1980 to 1985 periods. The average annual rate of change increased in the five-year period from 1990 to 1995. The rate increased both in terms of change in per member giving in inflation-adjusted dollars and as a percent of the average annual income increase.

Per Member Giving as Percentage of Income, 1921, 1933 and 1995. By 1995, U.S. per capita disposable (after-tax) personal income had increased 319%, in inflation-adjusted 1992 dollars, since 1921, and 404% since 1933—the depth of the Great Depression.

Meanwhile, by 1995, per member giving in inflation-adjusted 1992 dollars had increased 245% since 1921, and 266% since the depth of the Great Depression.

Consequently, per member giving as a percentage of income was lower in 1995 than in either 1921 or 1933. In 1921, per member giving as a percentage of income was 2.9%. In 1933, it was 3.3%. In 1995, per member giving as a percentage of income was 2.4% for the composite of the eleven denominations considered in this section. Thus, the percent change in the per member portion of income donated to the church had declined by 18% from the 1921 base, from 2.9% in 1921 to 2.4% in 1995, and by 27% from the 1933 base, from 3.3% in 1933 to 2.4% in 1995.

Appendix A contains a listing of the denominations contained in this analysis.

Summary. For a group of 11 Protestant denominations, giving as a percentage of income was above 3% of U.S. per capita disposable personal income from 1922 through 1933. It dropped below 3% in the later part of the Great Depression and reached a low point during World War II. The level of giving improved until it reached a high in 1960, when it began to decline.

During the years 1921-1995, the longest sustained period of increase in per member giving in inflation-adjusted 1992 dollars was 1947 to 1968. The next longest period was 1975-1995.

Per member giving and U.S. per capita disposable personal income, both in inflation-adjusted 1992 dollars, were analyzed in five-year increments for the years 1950-1995. The data indicates there was a marked decline in the rate of giving increase in the 1960-1964 period.

The data also indicates that giving as a portion of income was higher in both 1921 and 1933 than in 1995.

5

Church Member Giving and Membership Trends Based on 1968-1995 Data

Thirty years from now, how many vehicles will be using a highway that is currently on an engineer's drawing board? How many kindergartners will enroll in a community's public schools 25 years from now? What cumulative effect on the ozone layer will fluorocarbons have if present use levels continue through the end of the next century?

Calculations indicating the possible extinction of certain animal species led to hunting moratoriums. In response, for example, by 1995 the giant blue whale had reestablished itself.

Statistical analyses help concerned leaders address issues that will affect the quality of life for future generations 25 or 100 years from now. Such projections can be used to take certain factors into account, as in the case of future vehicle usage. Such projections can also encourage changes in present behaviors to produce an alternative outcome than the one predicted, such as in the case of the blue whale.

Statistical techniques can be used to suggest both consequences and possibilities regarding church giving and membership patterns as well. This type of trend analysis is useful in considering what data suggests the future will look like if the patterns of the past three decades continue in an uninterrupted fashion.

The Meaning of Trends. Linear regression and exponential regression are both standard statistical techniques that can be used to provide trend projections. The results of such analyses should be evaluated with the realization that these types of projections indicate—rather than dictate—future directions. For example, in the present church member giving analysis, the data can be used to develop giving trends that suggest what giving will look like in coming decades. These trends only indicate the present general direction of giving. Various factors—such as intentional education efforts by congregations and/or denominations, or spiritual renewal, or a decided loss of commitment to the church— could change giving patterns in unforeseen ways, either positively or negatively. Trends, therefore, are based on the assumption that either current conditions will remain constant or present suppositions regarding the future are valid. The trends point out the future of giving, if patterns continue without interruption. With those considerations in mind, one may explore what implications present data patterns have for the future.

The reason this analysis was first conducted resulted from present church conditions. After talking with numerous denominational officials who were making painful decisions about which programs to cut, in light of decreased Benevolences dollars being received, it seemed useful to see where the present patterns of giving might lead if effective means were not found to alter present behavior. Were current patterns likely to prove a temporary setback, or did the data suggest longer-term implications?

The Current Trend in Church Giving. The first chapter in this report indicates that per member giving as a percentage of income has been decreasing over a 28-year period. Further, contributions to the category of Benevolences have been declining proportionately faster than those to Congregational Finances between 1968 and 1995.

The data for the composite 29 denominations analyzed for 1968 through 1995 has been projected in *The State of Church Giving* series, beginning with the edition that included 1991 data.[12] The most recent projection includes data from 1968 through 1995.

The data for both Benevolences and Congregational Finances can be projected using linear and exponential regression analysis. To determine which type of analysis more accurately describes the data in a category's giving patterns, the data for 1968-1985 was projected using both techniques. Then, the actual data for 1986 through 1995 was plotted. The more accurate projection was judged to be the technique which produced the trend line that most closely resembled the actual 1986-1995 data.

The Trend in Benevolences. Of the two subcategories within Total Contributions, that is, Congregational Finances and Benevolences, the more pronounced negative trend occurred in Benevolences. Between 1968 and 1995, per member contributions to Benevolences as a percentage of income decreased from 0.66% in 1968 to 0.41% in 1995, a percent change in giving as a percentage of income of -38% from the 1968 base. In contrast, the percent change in giving as a percentage of income to Congregational Finances declined 16% from the 1968 base, from 2.46% in 1968 to 2.06% in 1995.

The data for giving as a percentage of income to Benevolences for the 17-year interval of 1968 through 1985 was projected using both linear and exponential regression. The actual data for 1986 through 1995 was also included. The results are shown in Figure 7.

The actual data for giving as a percentage of income to Benevolences for 1986 to 1995 followed the linear regression line more closely than the exponential curve. That would suggest that, if the giving patterns of the past 28 years continue in an uninterrupted fashion, then per member giving as a portion of income to the category of Benevolences will reach 0% of income in the year A.D. 2045.[13] In that year, the amount of income going to support

---

[12] John Ronsvalle and Sylvia Ronsvalle, *The State of Church Giving through 1991* (Champaign, IL: empty tomb, inc., 1993), and subsequent editions in the series. The edition with data through 1991 provides a discussion of the choice to use giving as a percentage of income as a basis for considering where present giving patterns might go in the future.

[13] The value for the correlation coefficient, or r_{XY}, for the Benevolences data is -.98. The strength of the linear relationship in the present set of 1968-1995 data, that is, the proportion of variance accounted for by linear regression, is represented by the coefficient of determination, or r^2_{XY}, of .96 for Benevolences. The Benevolences F-observed value of 677.00 is substantially greater than the F-critical value of 7.72 for 1 and 26 degrees of freedom for a single-tailed test with an Alpha value of 0.01. Therefore, the regression equation is useful at the level suggested by the r^2_{XY} figure in predicting giving as a percentage of income.

Figure 7:   Projected Trends for 29 Denominations, Giving as a Percentage of Income to Benevolences, Using Linear and Exponential Regression Based on Data for 1968-1985, with Actual Data for 1986-1995

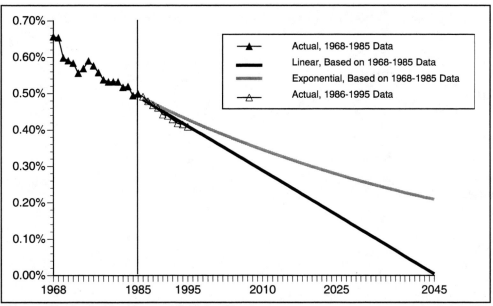

Sources: *Yearbook of American and Canadian Churches,*
adjusted series; U.S. Bureau of Economic Analysis

empty tomb, inc. 1997

those categories of expenditures within the definition of Benevolences, including denominational structures, would be negligible if current patterns hold constant.

The Trend in Congregational Finances. The church giving data contained in this report indicated that, while there was a less pronounced trend in Congregational Finances, giving as a percentage of income also declined between 1968 and 1995 to that category.

Once again, both linear and exponential regression were used to analyze the data for giving as a percentage of income to Congregational Finances for the 17-year interval of 1968 through 1985. The actual data for 1986 through 1995 was also included. The results are shown in Figure 8.

In the case of giving as a percentage of income to Congregational Finances, the actual data for 1986-1995 was closer to the exponential curve than to the linear regression line. That data suggests that by the year 2050, a few years after Benevolences are expected to represent 0% of members' incomes, giving to Congregational Finances will be at 1.39%, down from 2.06% in 1995, a decrease of 32% in the portion of income donated to support the activities of the congregations.

Membership in the Composite 29 Denominations, 1968-1995. Earlier chapters discuss the patterns in church member giving in a composite of 29 denominations. How does membership for this group of denominations fare in addition to giving patterns?

This group of denominations which span the theological spectrum included 28,163,801 Full or Confirmed Members in 1968. By 1995, these communions included 30,582,730

Figure 8: **Projected Trends for 29 Denominations, Giving as a Percentage of Income to Congregational Finances, Using Linear and Exponential Regression Based on Data for 1968-1985, with Actual Data for 1986-1995**

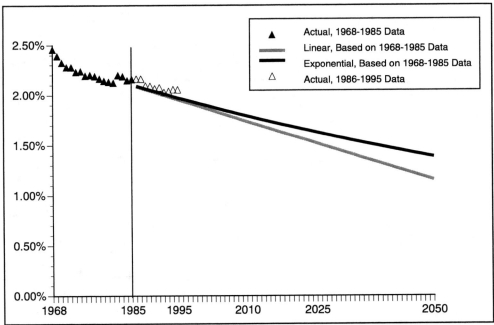

Sources: *Yearbook of American and Canadian Churches,* adjusted series; U.S. Bureau of Economic Analysis

empty tomb, inc. 1997

members, an increase of 9%.[14] However, during the same 28-year period, U.S. population had increased from 200,745,000 to 263,090,000, an increase of 31%. Therefore, while this grouping represented 14% of the U.S. population in 1968, it included 12% in 1995. Figure 9 presents per member giving as a percentage of income as well as membership as a percentage of U.S. population for these 29 denominations.

Trends in Church Membership as a Percentage of U.S. Population.[15] *The State of Church Giving through 1993* includes a chapter entitled, "A Unified Theory of Giving and Membership." The hypothesis explored in that discussion is that there is a relationship between a decline in church member giving and membership patterns. One proposal considered in that chapter is that a denomination which is able to involve its members in a larger vision as evidenced in giving patterns will also be attracting additional members.

In the present edition, discussion will be limited to patterns and trends in membership as a percentage of U.S. population.

---

[14] Since membership data was not available for the Friends United Meeting as of 1990, that group is not included in the membership data. Consult Appendix B-4 for the Full or Confirmed Membership used for the American Baptist Churches in the U.S.A., as well as the membership data for other denominations included in subsequent analyses in this chapter which are not included in the 29 denominations.

[15] The denominations analyzed in this section include the composite of 29 communions analyzed elsewhere in this report. The data for 29 communions is supplemented by the data of 9 denominations included in an analysis of church membership and U.S. population by Roozen and Hadaway in David A. Roozen and Kirk C. Hadaway, eds., *Church and Denominational Growth* (Nashville: Abingdon Press, 1993), 393-395.

Figure 9: **Giving as a Percentage of Income and Membership as a Percentage of U.S. Population, 29 Denominations, 1968-1995**

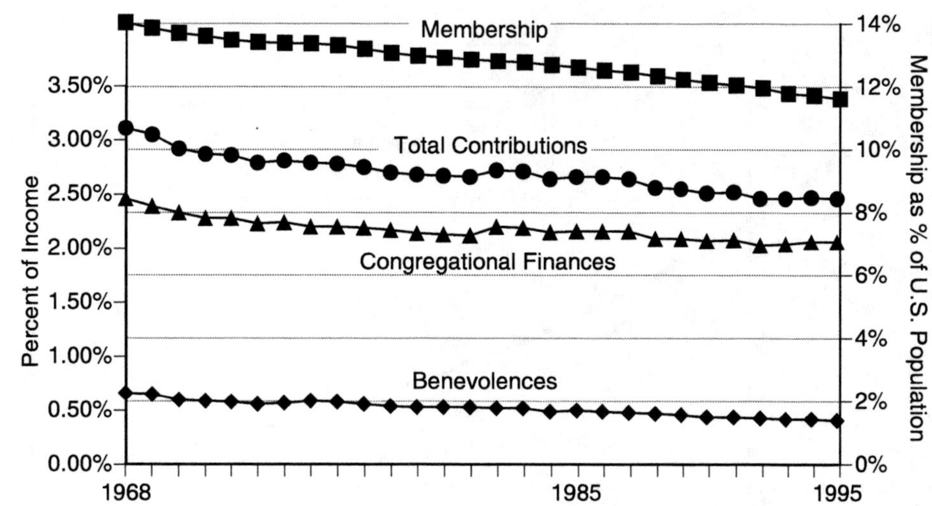

Sources: *Yearbook of American and Canadian Churches,*
adjusted series; U.S. Bureau of Economic Analysis

empty tomb, inc. 1997

Membership in Ten Mainline Denominations. The declining membership trends have been noticed most markedly in the mainline Protestant communions. Full or confirmed membership in ten mainline Protestant denominations affiliated with the National Council of the Churches of Christ in the U.S.A.[16] decreased as a percentage of U.S. population by 40% between 1968 and 1995. In 1968, this group included 26,390,858, or 13.1% of U. S. population. In 1995, the group included 20,573,566, or 7.8% of U.S. population.

As with giving as a percentage of income to Congregational Finances and Benevolences, the 1968-1985 membership data for these ten mainline Protestant communions was analyzed using both linear and exponential regression. The actual 1986 through 1995 data was also presented. As shown in Figure 10, the actual 1986-1995 data more closely follows the exponential curve. The data would therefore suggest that these ten denominations will represent 2.69% of the U.S. population by the year 2050, a decrease of 66% from the 1995 level of 7.82%.

Membership Trends in the 29 Denominations. Eight of the ten mainline Protestant denominations discussed above are included in the composite of 29 denominations that have been considered in earlier chapters of this report. Regression analysis was carried out on the 1968-1985 data for this grouping of 29 denominations to determine if the trends in the larger grouping differ from the mainline denominations. The results were then compared to the actual 1986 through 1995 membership data for the group of 29 denominations.

---

[16] These ten denominations include 8 of the communions in the composite of 29 denominations as well as data for The Episcopal Church and The United Methodist Church. The Friends United Meeting data is not considered in the membership projections, since data was not available after 1990 for that communion.

Figure 10: **Trend in Membership as a Percent of U.S. Population, Ten Mainline Protestant Denominations, Linear and Exponential Regression Based on Data for 1968-1985, with Actual Data 1986-1995**

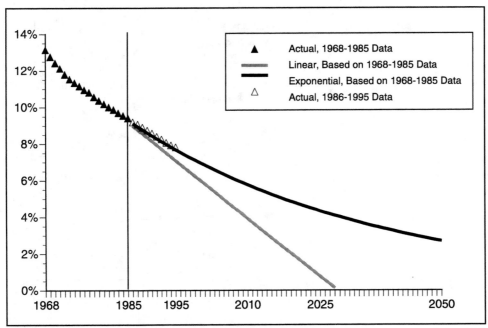

Sources: *Yearbook of American and Canadian Churches,* adjusted series; U.S. Bureau of Economic Analysis

empty tomb, inc. 1997

The 29 denominations represented 14% of the U.S. population in 1968, and 12.6% in 1985. Linear trend analysis suggests that this grouping would have represented 11.80% of U.S. population in 1995, while exponential regression suggests it would have been 11.87%. In fact, this grouping of 29 communions represented 11.62% of the U.S. population in 1995, a smaller figure than that indicated by linear regression, suggesting the trend is closer to that predicted by linear regression than the exponential curve.

If the trend of the last 28 years, from 1968-1995, continues uninterrupted into the future, these 29 denominations would represent 7.6% of the U.S. population in the year 2050, and 0% in the year 2150. This points to a decrease of 46% from 1968 levels in membership as a percent of U.S. population by the year 2050 for this set of communions. Figure 11 presents this information in graphic form.

Membership in an Expanded Set of Communions. In addition to these 29 denominations, membership data for the period 1968-1995 is available for several additional Protestant communions as well, bringing the number of Protestant denominations with available data to 36. This expanded set of denominations includes some of the fastest growing denominations in the U.S. When one considers whether the Protestant church in the U.S. is being marginalized as a social institution, a larger grouping of denominations would provide a broader base from which to gain additional insight.

In 1968, these 36 Protestant denominations represented 42,629,775 members, and in 1995, a total of 43,573,985, an increase of 2%. Meanwhile, the overall population in the U.S. had been growing at a faster rate than the membership changes posted by these denominations. As a result, these communions were 21% of the U.S. population in 1968, and 17% in 1995.

Figure 11: **Trend in Membership as a Percent of U.S. Population, 29 Protestant Denominations, Linear and Exponential Regression Based on Data for 1968-1985, with Actual Data 1986-1995**

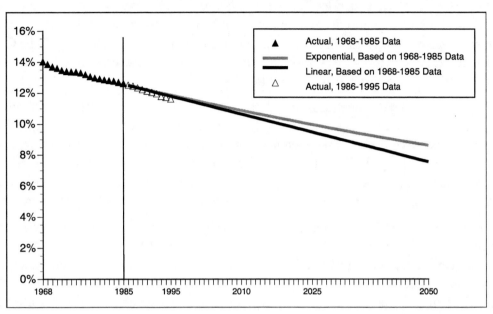

Sources: *Yearbook of American and Canadian Churches,* adjusted series; U.S. Bureau of Economic Analysis   empty tomb, inc. 1997

Of course, the picture would be incomplete without the Roman Catholic Church. Adding this membership data to that of the 36 Protestant communions considered above resulted in a total of 90,098,108 members in 1968. With the U.S. population at 200,745,000, these Christians constituted 45% of the 1968 U.S. population. By 1995, the group had grown to 103,854,439 members. However, with U.S. population having grown to 263,090,000, as of 1995, these Christians comprised 39% of the American population, a 12% decrease from the 1968 base.

The Response to the Trends. As in other sectors, trend lines in church giving and membership are designed to provide another source of information. Planning, evaluation and creative thinking are some of the types of constructive responses which can be made in light of projections. The information on church member giving and membership trends is offered as a possible planning tool.[17] The trend lines are not considered to be dictating what must happen, but rather as providing important indicators of what might happen if present conditions continue in an uninterrupted fashion. The results of the analysis may be useful as additional input to inform decisions by church leaders in the present.

The data reflects trends that raise important implications for the future. One might liken the projection to a symptom of illness. If a person is running a temperature of 104°, the choice would be to call the doctor or hope the fever runs its course. In either case, the body is communicating that there is a condition present which requires attention. Trends in church

---

[17] For additional discussion of the implications of the trends, see Ronsvalle and Ronsvalle, *The State of Church Giving through 1991*, pp. 61-67.

giving and membership, if used wisely, may be of assistance in addressing conditions present in the body of Christ in the U.S.

The Potential of the Church. Trends can also be used to review historical data and calculate possibilities of what might have happened under other circumstances. For example, in chapter one, consideration is given to per member giving between 1968 and 1995. The final section of that chapter reviews the amount of money that would have been given if 1995 giving levels had been the same as they were in 1968.

With the current national discussion about welfare reform, for example, the topic of whether the private sector can take responsibility for the support of individuals who had previously received government assistance has been hotly debated. One national nonprofit leader estimated that the private sector would have to cover an additional $15.7 billion annually to replace government cuts to programs that serve needy families. The leader pointed out that this amount is more than twice that currently given toward human services.[18]

Certainly, current giving patterns in the church, as well as other charitable giving information, would support the conclusion that the private sector does not presently have the money to absorb government cuts to welfare programs. The question may be asked, however, whether the private sector, or more specifically the sector presently under review which is the historically Christian church in the U.S., would potentially have the resources to absorb such cuts.

The Giving Rate from 1946 to 1960. In a review of giving patterns in 11 Protestant denominations, it was noted that church member giving sustained a long period of increase during the years from 1946 through 1960. What if giving, not only for these 11 denominations but also for a broader cross section of the church, had continued to increase at that post-World War II rate? The result would have been that, instead of giving at the 2.46% level in 1995, the members of the 29 communions in the composite data set would have been giving 6.08% in 1995. This amount is higher than the 1995 average of 4.08% for the eight denominations affiliated with the National Association of Evangelicals considered in an earlier chapter of this report. However, there are individual denominations that reported 1995 giving levels that were higher than 6.08% in the *Yearbook of American and Canadian Churches*.

The practical implications of this difference is that instead of giving $15 billion to their churches in 1995, the members of these denominations would have given $37 billion that year. The potential difference would have been $22 billion.

One may continue this hypothetical discussion by supposing that this additional money could have been directed not to the internal operations of the congregations, but rather to the broader mission of the church. Finally, one may suppose that denominations had adopted a proposed formula that 60% of this additional money be designated for international

---

[18] Fred Kammer, SJ, "Government Has a Responsibility to Poor Families," *The NonProfit Times*, July 1997, 50.

missions, and 20% be directed to domestic benevolences.[19] In this scenario, the 60% allocation would have meant in 1995 there would have been an additional $13 billion available for international outreach through the 29 denominations, and the 20% allocation would have meant an additional $4 billion for domestic benevolences.

A Rate Equal to Income Increases for Giving to Religion. Another analysis could be based on the supposition that giving could have increased at the rate of change in U.S. disposable personal income between 1968 and 1995. If that had been the case, the rate of giving in 1995 as a percentage of income for the 29 denominations would not have been 2.46%, but rather 5.22%. The theoretical level of giving as a percentage of income would have been 212% of what it actually was in 1995.

In the chapter that compares various sources of giving estimates, a revised series of giving to religion is offered. This 1968-1995 series is keyed to the 1974 Filer Commission estimate of giving to religion. The 1968-1995 annual rate of change in the composite 29 denominations was used to calculate figures for 1968-1973 and forward for 1975-1995, thus producing estimates of giving to religion. The result is that the 1995 estimate for total giving to religion was $44.5 billion.

Had giving to religion increased at a rate commensurate with the changes in income, the total amount of giving to religion in 1995 would have been 212% greater than the $44.5 billion figure. Therefore, instead of $44.5 billion given to religion in 1995, the amount would have been $94.2 billion. The additional amount of giving to religion in 1995 at that rate would have been $49.7 billion.

It is estimated that 84% of the U.S. population identifies with the historically Christian church.[20] Applying that percentage to total giving to religion, historically Christian church members would have given an additional $41.8 billion dollars to their churches in 1995, if the portion of income given had increased at the same rate as income.

Once again using the formulation that 60% of this money could have gone to international mission, and 20% to domestic benevolences, then there would have been $25 billion additional for international outreach, and $8.4 billion additional for domestic outreach.

Growing Toward the Tithe. Although the pros and cons of the practice continue to be discussed within church circles, the classic tithe, or giving 10% of one's income, has been a standard throughout the history of the church.

In considering what might have happened in church giving, at least two more scenarios can be considered. One scenario can be developed based on the 1968 giving level

---

[19] UNICEF estimates that 35,000 children under the age of five die daily around the globe, mostly from preventable poverty conditions. UNICEF also estimates that 40,000 children under the age of five die annually in the United States. These statistics indicate that the great majority of need is in countries other than the U.S. The 60%/20% formula has been used in the authors' work with congregations. For a discussion of their international and domestic strategy approaches, see John Ronsvalle and Sylvia Ronsvalle, *The Poor Have Faces* (Grand Rapids, MI: Baker Books, 1992).

[20] An analysis based on information in: George H. Gallup, Jr., *Religion in America* (Princeton, NJ: The Princeton Religion Research Center, 1996), 42.

in the 29 denominations growing to 10% by the year 2050. The other can be developed on the hypothetical situation that giving had increased from the 1968 level to 10% by 1995.

In the first scenario, giving would have increased from 3.11% in 1968 to 10% in the year 2050. On the way toward that goal, giving would have been 5.38% in 1995, rather than the 2.46% it actually was. This revised level of giving is 218% higher than the actual level.

Again, applying that 218% to the calculated $44.5 billion that was given to religion in 1995, the revised total would have been $97 billion. The increased level of giving would have been $53 billion. Of this theoretical increase, $44 billion would have been contributed by members of historically Christian churches. The 60% of this additional giving directed to international ministries would have been $26.5 billion. The 20% of the additional amount available, to be directed to domestic benevolences, would have been $8.8 billion.

In the second scenario, giving would have increased from 3.11% in 1968 to 10% in 1995. This level of income being donated to the church would be 406% greater than the actual 1995 level of 2.46%. At that rate, instead of $44 billion donated to religion in 1995, the amount would have been $180 billion, an increase of $136 billion.

Applying the 84% figure to the $136 billion increase, there would have been $114 billion additional donated in 1995 by those who claim affiliation with the historically Christian church, had average giving been at the 10% level. The international amount, at the 60% level, would have been $68.5 billion, more than the $30-$50 billion annually UNICEF has estimated is needed to address the worst of poverty conditions and end most of the child deaths around the globe.[21] The 20% available for domestic benevolences would have amounted to $22.8 billion.

Figure 12 presents the three scenarios of potential church giving.

The Implications of the Hypothetical Scenarios. As the nonprofit sector receives more attention from society in general, the role it plays and can play is discussed and debated. One might review the above scenarios in order to consider the question of whether the private sector, or more specifically the church, can take on additional responsibilities toward those who are in need in the U.S.

The data suggests that, if giving had increased from the actual 1995 level to an average level of 10%, there could have been an additional $22.8 billion available for domestic needs. In theory, therefore, the church could have the resources necessary to impact domestic need, even while working at a significant level to alleviate global need in partnership with international sister churches.

If giving had increased between 1968 and 1995 at the same rate as income did, or if it was increasing toward a level of 10% giving, the church would have had over $8 billion more in 1995 for domestic benevolences, and could have been seriously considered as a significant source of servanthood leadership for addressing poverty issues in the U.S.

This potential should not be ignored in the ongoing discussions.

However, it should also be noted that giving as a percentage of income did not increase at the rate that income did between 1968 and 1995, it was not increasing toward 10%

---

[21] James P. Grant, *The State of the World's Children 1990* (New York, Oxford University Press, 1989), 67.

Figure 12: **1995 Potential Additional Church Giving, including International and Domestic Allocations: at a Rate Equal to U.S. Per Capita Disposable Personal Income Changes; at a Rate to Reach 10% by 2050; at an Average of 10%**

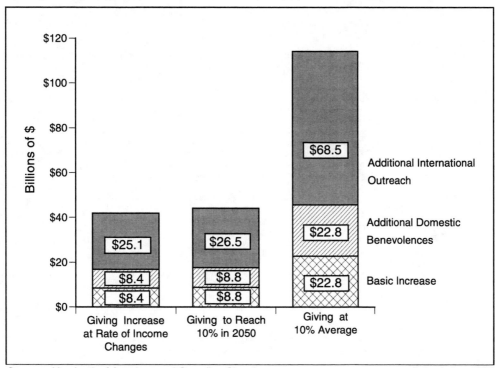

Sources: *Yearbook of American and Canadian Churches,* adjusted series; U.S. Bureau of Economic Analysis

empty tomb, inc. 1997

at some point in the future, nor had it reached the 10% level by 1995. On the contrary, giving as a percentage of income declined by 21% between 1968 and 1995. More to the point, the portion of income going to Benevolences, the category that would take into account programs that address poverty issues in the U.S. among other issues, declined by 38% in the 1968 to 1995 period.

One may conclude that although the church has the potential for making a larger impact than it currently is doing, church members are apparently not interested in doing so. The implications of that conclusion are explored in the last chapter of this report.

Summary. The results of trend analysis do not dictate future behavior patterns, but rather only indicate where present patterns are headed.

Giving to Benevolences as a percentage of income closely parallels a linear regression trend line, while giving to Congregational Finances follows an exponential curve more closely.

Church membership is declining as a percentage of U.S. population. The pattern is evident in a group of 10 mainline denominations, in the data set of 29 denominations, and in an expanded group that includes 36 Protestant denominations and the Roman Catholic Church.

Had church giving expanded at the rate that incomes did between 1968 and 1995, or toward an average of 10%, the church would have had billions of additional dollars available to apply to domestic benevolences. In contrast to this hypothetical analysis, actual data indicates that church member giving as a percentage of income declined during the 1968 to 1995 period.

6

Denominational Reports and Other Estimates of Charitable Giving_____

How much money is donated to charitable causes in the United States each year?

That question seems like it should have a fairly simple answer. There are two main estimates that are widely reported. However, upon closer inspection, questions arise about what these sources actually convey. One widely quoted figure is the result of a formula that produces a projection, rather than a statistic based on external aggregated data. The other information source suggests that charitable giving is quite volatile, in contrast to reports from various agency sources that suggest it is fairly stable.

The questions about these estimates of giving have broader implications than confirming an academic number. For example, government policy discussions that affect the lives of people—such as welfare reform debates about whether the private sector can absorb the responsibility for the well-being of those in need—may rely on these estimates to help form policy. Therefore, understanding how current giving estimates are generated is important for many reasons beyond academic integrity.

Before considering estimates of giving to religion, it may be helpful to review how one widely-cited estimate is developed.

American Association of Fund-Raising Counsel (AAFRC) Giving USA Methodology. An often-quoted source of charitable giving data is the *Giving USA* series produced by the American Association of Fund-Raising Counsel, Inc. Trust for Philanthropy (AAFRC). These annual reports include an estimate for total charitable giving in the United States. The total figure includes a subtotal for individual charitable giving, which comprises about 80% of total charitable giving. The reports also include separate estimates for charitable donations by use, such as religion, human services, and health.

What is not widely understood is that the estimate of individual charitable giving is a calculation that is independent of the estimates of charitable giving by use. That is, AAFRC actually produces two different sets of numbers, using two different methodologies, and then tries to match them. The estimate for the amount of money given by individuals, is developed by an econometric model, while the use categories estimates are developed by a combination of approaches.

A difference between the total that is calculated to have been donated, which includes the amount for individual giving resulting from the econocentric model, and the amount that is calculated to have been received in the different use categories occurs. The AAFRC staff has applied different methods over the years to deal with the difference between the projected amount given and the combined amount estimated to have been received by the use categories. For data beginning at some unstated point and continuing through 1986, any difference between the individual giving projection and the sum of the other use categories was deposited in the use category of religion, which was regarded as a "residual" category.[22] More recently, differences were attributed, at least in part, to a category labeled alternatively "Unallocated," "All Other Uses," "Undesignated" or "Unclassified."

There is also a third charitable giving estimate prepared by AAFRC, in that AAFRC routinely revises its recent historical series, as additional tax and other information is available.

AAFRC has been working to improve its estimates of giving. Since 1993, AAFRC revised its methodology regarding estimates of individual giving once again. As of the 1997 edition of *Giving USA*, revisions were made for the period 1984-1994. The years 1995 and 1996 were projections, because needed information for the revisions was not yet available.[23]

AAFRC also has striven to improve its use estimates. AAFRC incorporates surveys of service agencies to project a figure for many of its use categories, such as education, health and human services. In addition, in 1989 AAFRC presented revised historical estimates for the categories of education and health. In these cases, AAFRC stated that it keyed the 1960-1972 estimates for these categories to estimates developed by the Commission on Private Philanthropy and Public Needs, commonly referred to as the Filer Commission.[24] The Filer Commission was a major national effort that resulted in a report published by the U.S. Treasury Department. According to that report, "There had been no full-scale national surveys of philanthropy prior to this study."[25] Thus, AAFRC relied on the Filer Commission estimates to provide a reference point for its historical series in the second and third largest areas of charitable activity.

Giving to Religion, Denomination-Based Series Compared to AAFRC Series. Religion is acknowledged as the single largest use category in the charitable arena. Estimates suggest almost 60% of every charitable dollar donated by individuals is designated for religion.[26] If donations to other organizations that have a religious affiliation but appear in

---

[22] Nathan Weber, *Giving USA 1990*, (New York: AAFRC Trust for Philanthropy, 1990), 187. AAFRC indicated that it revised its 1987 through 1995 data in "Methodology" 17-6 (see note 2 below for citation).

[23] "Methodology" ([New York: American Association of Fund Raising Counsel, Inc., 1997]), 17-4.

[24] Nathan Weber, ed., *Giving USA 1989* (New York: AAFRC Trust for Philanthropy, 1989), 151.

[25] James N. Morgan, Richard F. Due, Judith N. Hybels, "Results from Two National Surveys of Philanthropic Activity," *History, Trends, and Current Magnitudes*, Vol. 1 in the series, *Research Papers Sponsored by The Commission on Private Philanthropy and Public Needs*, Department of the Treasury, Washington, DC, 1977, 158.

[26] AAFRC estimates that religion received 59% of individual charitable giving in 1995 ($66.26 billion of a total individual giving level of $112.22) [Ann E. Kaplan, ed., *Giving USA 1997* (New York: AAFRC Trust for Philanthropy, 1997), 198, 200] , while Independent Sector found that 57.5% of individual giving went to religious organizations (Virginia A. Hodgkinson and Murray S. Weitzman, *Giving and Volunteering in the United States, 1996* (Washington, DC: Independent Sector, 1996), 25].

another use category—such as the Salvation Army or Catholic Social Services that are part of human services—were also considered, the portion of giving that is a function of religious activity would be even higher.[27] Therefore, having an accurate estimate of giving to religion is important in determining the level of charitable financial activity in the U.S.

The Filer Commission produced an estimate of giving to religion. That report estimated that in 1974, giving to religion was $11.7 billion.[28] This estimate was close to the AAFRC estimate for 1974 of $11.84 billion.[29]

When revising its historical series, AAFRC did not choose to key its religion data to the Filer Commission estimate of giving to religion.

AAFRC did revise its religion estimates for 1987 through 1995 based on the percent change in receipts for a set of denominations that publish data in the *Yearbook of American and Canadian Churches* series.[30]

In theory, one could follow a methodology for religion similar to that AAFRC used for the categories of education and health, in this case keying 1974 to the Filer Commission estimate, and then calculate estimates for the years 1968 to 1973, and 1975 to 1995, based on an external source of data. The external source of data could be the same that AAFRC used to revise its 1987 through 1995 data, a set of denominations that publish data in the *Yearbook of American and Canadian Churches* series. This revised approach would remedy the estimates for those years when AAFRC did not calculate a figure for religion, but rather considered it a "residual" category, having the use category of religion absorb the difference between AAFRC's estimate of total giving and the sum of its estimates for other use categories.

The starting base in this approach could be the Filer Commission estimate of $11.7 billion for 1974. The amount of change from year to year, calculated for 1968 to 1973 and also 1975 to 1995, could be the annual percentage change in the 29 denominations analyzed in other chapters of this report. This calculation yields a total of $8 billion given to religion in 1968, and $44.5 billion in 1995. These figures contrast with the AAFRC estimate of $8.42 billion in 1968 and $66.26 billion in 1995. Table 16 presents this data.

Comparing these two estimate series, one may observe that the two series are within a few percentage points of each other for two years on either side of 1974, the year of the Filer

---

[27] For a discussion of the definition of religious charitable contributions, see Ronsvalle and Ronsvalle, "Denominational Giving Data and Other Sources of Religious Giving Information," *The State of Church Giving through 1991* (Champaign, IL: empty tomb, inc., 1993), 53-57.

[28] *Research Papers Sponsored by The Commission on Private Philanthropy and Public Needs, Vol. 1, History, Trends, and Current Magnitudes*, Department of the Treasury, Washington, DC, 1977, 136.

[29] Ann E. Kaplan, *Giving USA 1993* (New York: American Association of Fund-Raising Counsel Trust for Philanthropy, 1993), 22.

[30] AAFRC suggests that its 1986 data matches that of other religion sources. The 1986 estimate is close to the estimate in the first edition of the Independent Sector report, *From Belief to Commitment* by Virginia A. Hodgkinson, Murray Weitzman, and Arthur D. Kirsch, eds. (Washington, DC: Independent Sector, 1988). However, the next Independent Sector figure in Virginia A. Hodgkinson, Murray Weitzman, et al., *From Belief to Commitment* (Washington, DC: Independent Sector, 1992) varied from the AAFRC estimate. For a discussion of the latter data, see Ronsvalle and Ronsvalle, *The State of Church Giving through 1991*, 41-42.

Table 16: **Giving to Religion, AAFRC Series and Denomination-Based Series, 1968-1995, Aggregate, Billions of Dollars and Percent Difference**

Year	AAFRC Series (Billions $)	Denomination-Based Series Keyed to 1974 Filer Series (Billions $)	Percent Difference between AAFRC and Denomination-Based Series
1968	$8.42	$8.0	5%
1969	$9.02	$8.4	7%
1970	$9.34	$8.6	9%
1971	$10.07	$9.1	11%
1972	$10.10	$9.8	3%
1973	$10.53	$10.7	-2%
1974	$11.84	$11.7	1%
1975	$12.81	$12.8	0%
1976	$14.18	$13.9	2%
1977	$16.98	$15.1	12%
1978	$18.35	$16.4	12%
1979	$20.17	$18.1	11%
1980	$22.23	$20.0	11%
1981	$25.05	$22.1	13%
1982	$28.06	$24.0	17%
1983	$31.84	$25.7	24%
1984	$35.55	$27.8	28%
1985	$38.21	$29.6	29%
1986	$41.68	$31.0	34%
1987	$43.51	$32.5	34%
1988	$45.15	$33.8	34%
1989	$47.77	$35.7	34%
1990	$49.79	$37.2	34%
1991	$53.92	$38.6	40%
1992	$54.91	$39.7	38%
1993	$56.29	$40.7	38%
1994	$60.21	$42.6	41%
1995	$66.26	$44.5	49%

Details in the above table may not compute to the numbers shown due to rounding.

estimate to which the denominational-based series is keyed. The estimates vary about 10% through 1981. AAFRC methodology does not indicate when religion became a residual use category, although the differences in the data series suggests some change in AAFRC methodology took place between 1976 and 1977.

In 1982, while the denominational-based estimate series continues to change at a consistent rate, the AAFRC estimate series begins to expand more rapidly from year to year. The percentage difference grew from 17% in 1982 to 49% in 1995.

Although AAFRC revised its data for 1987 through 1995 based on a different methodology than the residual definition, those latter estimates continued to build on the earlier years' data, during which religion was a residual category absorbing any difference between AAFRC's individual giving estimate and its sum of the other use category estimates.

Total Charitable Giving, Denomination-Based Series Compared to AAFRC Series. The historical series of denomination-based data keyed to the Filer Commission can be used to consider an alternative estimate of total charitable giving.

The use categories, other than religion, are generally based on surveys of large organizations within the activity definition, such as the Council for Aid to Education in the category of education, and the Association of Healthcare Philanthropy in the area of health. When such combined data is not available, according to the AAFRC methodology publication, AAFRC staff surveys organizations within the particular category.[31] These specific data are then extrapolated to represent the entire category.

One method for developing an alternative estimate to AAFRC's total charitable giving series would be first to sum the amount of the various AAFRC use categories, excluding religion. Rather than using the AAFRC historical series for religion, the denomination-based figures that are keyed to the Filer Commission 1974 estimate can then be added to the sum of the other use categories. In this way, a revised series is developed for total charitable giving, as shown in Table 17. One advantage of this revised series is that it is based on an explicit methodology for the important subcategory of religion.

As in the religion series comparison, the two series of figures remain very close from 1972 to 1976. The difference increases in 1977, and then the difference increases to more than 10% in 1983. The AAFRC series then continues to grow at a faster pace than the denomination-based series. In 1995, the difference between the series is 18%. The magnitude of the difference becomes apparent when that difference is considered in billions of dollars. The difference between the AAFRC estimates and the denomination-based series that includes the denomination-based estimate for religion, amounts to $21.79 billion, which is 15% of the entire charitable sector, using the base of $140.5 billion.

Individual Charitable Giving, Denomination-Based Series Compared to AAFRC Series. Individual giving makes up the major portion of giving to religion: "Most giving to religion comes from individuals. Some giving to religion also comes from bequests, and about two percent of foundation grants go to religion."[32] Therefore, while a revised series for religion affects the total charitable giving estimate, the effect would be more pronounced in the category of total individual giving, where, based on AAFRC estimates, more than fifty-five cents of every dollar is donated to religion.

To develop a revised estimate of individual giving, the AAFRC estimate of giving to religion can be subtracted from the AAFRC total of individual giving. This methodology is only approximate since, as AAFRC notes, some giving to religion comes from bequests—an amount not noted in the AAFRC methodology—and about 2% of foundation grants are also donated to religion. In 1995, at the 2% level, the foundation grants would have amounted

---

[31] "Methodology," 17-7.

[32] Ann E. Kaplan, ed., *Giving USA 1996* (New York: American Association of Fund-Raising Counsel Trust for Philanthropy, 1996), 101.

Table 17:   Total Charitable Giving, AAFRC Series and Revised Total Charitable Giving Series Using the Denomination-Based Religion Series, 1968-1995, Billions of Dollars and Percent Difference

Year	AAFRC Estimate Series (Billions $)	Revised Estimate Using Den.-Based Religion Series (Billions $)	Percent Difference between AAFRC and Revised Series
1968	$18.85	$18.48	2%
1969	$20.66	$19.99	3%
1970	$21.04	$20.29	4%
1971	$23.44	$22.51	4%
1972	$24.44	$24.13	1%
1973	$25.59	$25.76	-1%
1974	$26.88	$26.74	1%
1975	$28.56	$28.52	0%
1976	$31.85	$31.58	1%
1977	$35.21	$33.28	6%
1978	$38.57	$36.66	5%
1979	$43.11	$41.06	5%
1980	$48.63	$46.38	5%
1981	$55.28	$52.32	6%
1982	$59.11	$55.02	7%
1983	$63.21	$57.03	11%
1984	$68.58	$60.79	13%
1985	$72.96	$64.35	13%
1986	$83.79	$73.13	15%
1987	$89.99	$79.01	14%
1988	$98.13	$86.77	13%
1989	$106.73	$94.63	13%
1990	$111.47	$98.86	13%
1991	$117.22	$101.91	15%
1992	$121.09	$105.83	14%
1993	$126.46	$110.93	14%
1994	$129.27	$111.61	16%
1995	$140.45	$118.66	18%

Details in the above table may not compute to the numbers shown due to rounding.

to $211 million dollars.[33] Without more specific data about the source of contributions provided by AAFRC in its methodology, attributing 100% of religion to individual giving provides an initial basis for comparison.

---

[33] The 1995 AAFRC estimate for foundations was $10.56. Two percent of that amount would be $211 million dollars. Total bequests in 1995 are estimated to have been $9.77 billion. See Ann E. Kaplan, ed., *Giving USA 1997* (New York: American Association of Fund-Raising Counsel Trust for Philanthropy, 1997), 198.

The AAFRC giving to religion series was subtracted from the AAFRC individual giving series. The denomination-based series keyed to the Filer Commission estimate was then added to the resulting AAFRC individual series from which the AAFRC giving to religion series had been subtracted. The revised individual denomination-based giving series is compared to the original AAFRC individual giving series in Table 18.

Table 18:   **Individual Giving, AAFRC Series and Revised Individual Giving Series Using the Denomination-Based Religion Series, 1968-1995, Billions of Dollars and Percent Difference**

Year	AAFRC Estimate Series (Billions $)	Revised Estimate Using Denomination-Based Religion Series (Billions $)	Percent Difference between AAFRC and Revised Series
1968	$14.75	$14.38	3%
1969	$15.93	$15.26	4%
1970	$16.19	$15.44	5%
1971	$17.64	$16.71	6%
1972	$19.37	$19.06	2%
1973	$20.53	$20.70	-1%
1974	$21.60	$21.46	1%
1975	$23.53	$23.49	0%
1976	$26.32	$26.05	1%
1977	$29.55	$27.62	7%
1978	$32.10	$30.19	6%
1979	$36.59	$34.54	6%
1980	$40.71	$38.46	6%
1981	$45.99	$43.03	7%
1982	$47.63	$43.54	9%
1983	$52.06	$45.88	13%
1984	$56.46	$48.67	16%
1985	$58.66	$50.06	17%
1986	$67.63	$56.97	19%
1987	$72.32	$61.34	18%
1988	$80.07	$68.71	17%
1989	$87.75	$75.65	16%
1990	$91.15	$78.55	16%
1991	$96.10	$80.78	19%
1992	$98.38	$83.13	18%
1993	$102.13	$86.58	18%
1994	$103.83	$86.18	20%
1995	$112.22	$90.43	24%

Details in the above table may not compute to the numbers shown due to rounding.

Not surprisingly since the basic data being used to revise the individual giving series is the same that was used to revise total charitable giving, the AAFRC estimates and the series based on denomination data that is keyed to the Filer Commission remain similar until

1976. At that point, the AAFRC estimate begins expanding at a faster rate than the denomination-based series. By 1995, the difference between the two estimates is 24%.

The advantage of the revised series that includes the denomination-based religion estimate is that the large component of religion that comprises somewhat over 55% of total individual gifts, is based on data reported by over 100,000 of the estimated 350,000 religious congregations of any type in the United States.

The AAFRC Econocentric Model for Individual Giving. Each year, AAFRC announces new totals of charitable giving in the United States. Approximately 80% of the most recent total charitable giving figure—the portion that is attributed to individual giving—is based on an econocentric model which produces a projection that almost necessarily increases. Yet, the level of giving increase is announced as news.

For example, the press release for *Giving USA* began with the sentence "Charitable contributions of $150.70 billion in 1996 surpassed the previous year's total by close to $10 billion, according to *Giving USA 1997*."[34]

Further, a subtitle for the press release read, "*Giving USA*'s 42nd Report Finds Strong Economy Buoyed Charitable Impulse." In paragraph 1, the release reads, "The increase . . . is the welcome result of a strong economy during a year when the nation's attention was drawn to charitable giving and the nonprofit sector." In paragraph 3, the release notes, "The short-run annual change in giving, however, is mainly driven by the economy."

The headline and sentences following it may imply that AAFRC has access to charitable giving data or survey information which can be compared to the growth in the economy and thus produce the stated conclusions. Alternatively, a closer reading by those familiar with AAFRC methodology may suggest that the text is hinting at the econocentric model that AAFRC uses to develop its individual giving projection based not on external giving data for the most recent year, but rather on a formula that calculates how much Americans gave, assuming past patterns continued through the present. Nor does the press release state clearly that the announced changes are based on such an econocentric model, two key components of which are "total personal income, the factor given the most weight; Standard and Poors 500 Stock Index for the months of November and December."[35] Since these two factors are included in the projection formula, if the economy is good then, of necessity, AAFRC's individual giving projection, which comprises 80% of its total charitable contributions figure, must increase. Although the press release headline suggests an element of surprise in the upward trend, anyone familiar with the AAFRC econocentric model would anticipate no other result.

Further, the model had to be revised in the most recent year because of the unusually strong economy. "In 1997, the trust's advisors noted that extrapolating two years from the baseline, warranted a modification in the extrapolating model. This was particularly important because the two primary factors affecting annual changes in giving, income and

---

[34] "Giving Reaches $150.7 Billion, Increase Well Ahead of Inflation for Second Year as Nation Focuses on Voluntary Contributions, *Giving USA*'s 42nd Report Finds Strong Economy Buoyed Charitable Impulse," AAFRC Press Release (n.d.) [Online]. URL http://www.aafrc.org/NEWS.HTM.

[35] Kaplan, *Giving USA 1996*, 173.

the stock market, were both increasing strongly, and might cause an unreasonable projection using the standard model."[36]

Aggregate Versus Per Capita Data. The press release announcement also focuses on the aggregate total of giving amounts. Given the econocentric model, aggregate numbers for individual giving will necessarily increase from year to year in an expanding economy.

However, aggregate numbers do not take into account the element of population change. Commenting on the importance of reliable reporting, Philip Meyer notes:

> Trends make news . . . To focus on the newsworthy trend, you have to separate it from all the parallel trends in the background. Population growth is one secular trend that, like inflation, can make other trends be more or less than they seem.[37]

When the AAFRC data—the series as published rather than the revised denomination-based series discussed above—takes population into account, the positive trend noted from year to year is affected.

In current dollars, according to the AAFRC aggregate individual data, giving increased between 1968 and 1995 from $14.75 billion in 1968 to $112.22 in 1995. When those aggregate numbers are divided by the population, the figures also show an increase on a per capita basis. In 1968, according to this data, per capita giving was $73.48 and in 1995, it was $426.55. As indicated in Table 1, presented in chapter one of this report, church member giving in the 29 denominations also increased on a per member basis in current dollars between 1968 and 1995.

One telling indicator is how much a contribution represents of the individual's overall income. In this way, one might attribute a weight to the value that people place on charitable activity in the context of their total spending patterns.

In 1968, U.S. per capita disposable personal income in current dollars was $3,101, and in 1995 it was $20,214. Disposable personal income is the category of choice because it takes into account the change in personal taxes during the 1968-1995 period. Although AAFRC does consider individual giving as a portion of income, it uses personal income which does not reflect changes in the level of taxes paid by individuals donating to charity.[38]

Per Capita Individual Giving. When the per capita AAFRC estimate of individual giving is taken as a portion of income, it becomes apparent that in 1968, charitable giving represented 2.37% of each American's income, while in 1995 it represented 2.11%, a decline of 11% in the portion of U.S. per capita disposable personal income contributed to charity.

As shown in Table 19 below, if the revised series of individual giving—substituting the denomination-based series for the AAFRC estimate of giving to religion— is used, we find that per capita individual giving was $71.63 in 1968 and $343.74 in 1995. When these amounts are taken as a portion of U.S. per capita disposable personal income, the portion of

---

[36] "Methodology," 17-4.

[37] Philip Meyer, *The New Precision Journalism* (Bloomington, IN: Indiana University Press, 1991), 30.

[38] Kaplan, *Giving USA 1997*, 64.

per capita income donated to charity declined from 2.31% in 1968 to 1.70% in 1995, a decline of 26%.

Table 19 presents the AAFRC and denomination-based series of per capita individual giving, in current dollars and as a percent of income.

Table 19: **Individual Giving, AAFRC Series and Revised Individual Giving Series Using the Denomination-Based Religion Series, 1968-1995, Per Capita Current Dollars and as a Percent of U.S. Disposable Personal Income**

Year	Per Capita AAFRC Series	Per Capita AAFRC Series as % of Income	Per Capita Revised Series Using Den.-Based Religion	Per Capita Revised Series as % of Income
1968	$73.48	2.37%	$71.63	2.31%
1969	$78.58	2.38%	$75.29	2.28%
1970	$78.94	2.22%	$75.26	2.12%
1971	$84.93	2.23%	$80.45	2.11%
1972	$92.27	2.26%	$90.78	2.22%
1973	$96.87	2.12%	$97.65	2.14%
1974	$100.98	2.04%	$100.33	2.03%
1975	$108.94	2.02%	$108.76	2.02%
1976	$120.69	2.06%	$119.45	2.04%
1977	$134.14	2.10%	$125.40	1.96%
1978	$144.19	2.02%	$135.60	1.90%
1979	$162.55	2.06%	$153.44	1.95%
1980	$178.78	2.06%	$168.90	1.94%
1981	$199.97	2.08%	$187.11	1.95%
1982	$205.12	2.02%	$187.50	1.85%
1983	$222.17	2.06%	$195.81	1.81%
1984	$238.84	2.00%	$205.87	1.73%
1985	$245.94	1.95%	$209.89	1.66%
1986	$280.98	2.11%	$236.68	1.78%
1987	$297.78	2.14%	$252.59	1.82%
1988	$326.69	2.19%	$280.32	1.88%
1989	$354.68	2.25%	$305.77	1.94%
1990	$364.67	2.18%	$314.25	1.88%
1991	$380.31	2.21%	$319.66	1.85%
1992	$385.07	2.13%	$325.40	1.80%
1993	$395.41	2.12%	$335.21	1.80%
1994	$398.30	2.06%	$330.61	1.71%
1995	$426.55	2.11%	$343.74	1.70%

Details in the above table may not compute to the numbers shown due to rounding.

Per Capita Giving to Religion. The aggregate data in Table 16 was divided by U.S. population to produce a per capita figure for both the AAFRC giving to religion series and the denomination-based series. The two series were then converted to giving as a percentage of U.S. disposable personal income. The comparison is presented in Figure 13 below.

Figure 13: **Giving to Religion, AAFRC Series and Denomination-Based Series, 1968-1995, Per Capita as a Percentage of U.S. Per Capita Disposable Personal Income**

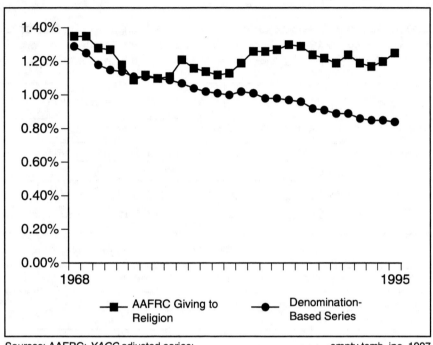

Sources: AAFRC; *YACC* adjusted series;   empty tomb, inc. 1997
U.S. BEA

Per Capita Giving to Other Use Categories, 1968-1995. The AAFRC aggregate use category totals are reported in a variety of settings. The Rand Corporation's Council for Aid to Education, for example, includes a chart using AAFRC data to indicate the levels of charitable giving by use and trends over time on its Web site.[39]

Once again, considering giving to various use categories on a per capita basis may provide a different picture than indicated by the aggregate data. A comparison is presented in Table 20 below.

It should be noted that the use categories presented by AAFRC do not make a distinction by source of contribution. AAFRC does state that the majority of donations to religion comes from individuals. However, AAFRC does not provide figures within each of the various use categories as to the amount of donations from each source, the four being: corporations, bequests, foundations, and individuals. Therefore, the comparison below is only approximate. It does, however, suggest important factors to be taken into consideration when discussing trends in charitable giving.

---

[39] "Distribution of Total Philanthropy by Cause," Council for Aid to Education (n.d.) [Online]. URL http://www.cae.org/trends/sk04.htm. For information about the relationship of the Rand Corporation to the Council for Aid to Education, URL http://www.cae.org/Aboutcae.htm and http://www.rand.org/facts/.

Table 20 presents data for the use categories of religion; education; health; human services; arts, culture, and humanities; and public/society benefit. Since data for the use categories of environment/wildlife and international affairs is provided only for years beginning with 1987, these categories are not included. The category of giving to foundations has data only back to 1988, and likewise is not considered in this table. The category of unclassified is also not included.

Table 20: **AAFRC Giving to Use Categories, 1968 and 1995, Aggregate, Current and Inflation-Adjusted 1996 Dollars (Billions $), and Per Capita as a Percent of U.S. Disposable Personal Income, with Percent Change 1968-1995**

	Religion			Education		
	Aggregate (Billions $)		Per Capita	Aggregate (Billions $)		Per Capita
	Current $	Infl.-Adj.'96 $	% Income	Current $	Infl.-Adj.'96 $	% Income
1968	$8.42	$41.29	1.35%	$2.38	$11.67	0.38%
1995	$66.26	$68.01	1.25%	$17.61	$18.07	0.33%
% Change	687%	65%	-8%	640%	55%	-13%

	Health			Human Services		
	Aggregate (Billions $)		Per Capita	Aggregate (Billions $)		Per Capita
	Current $	Infl.-Adj.'96 $	% Income	Current $	Infl.-Adj.'96 $	% Income
1968	$2.08	$10.20	0.33%	$2.31	$11.33	0.37%
1995	$12.59	$12.92	0.24%	$11.70	$12.01	0.22%
% Change	505%	27%	-29%	406%	6%	-41%

	Arts, Culture, and Humanities			Public/Society Benefit		
	Aggregate (Billions $)		Per Capita	Aggregate (Billions $)		Per Capita
	Current $	Infl.-Adj.'96 $	% Income	Current $	Infl.-Adj.'96 $	% Income
1968	$0.60	$2.96	0.10%	$0.43	$2.10	0.07%
1995	$9.96	$10.22	0.19%	$7.10	$7.29	0.13%
% Change	1560%	245%	94%	1551%	247%	93%

Details in the above table may not compute to the numbers shown due to rounding.

From this table, it is apparent once again that giving to religion receives the highest level of charitable giving support. Both aggregate giving and per capita giving to religion in current dollars increased. However, as a portion of U.S. per capita disposable personal income, the amount of giving to religion decreased by 8%. Table 20 uses the AAFRC estimate of giving to religion series. When the denomination-based series data was used instead, the portion of U.S. disposable personal income donated to religion declined from 1.29% in 1968 to 0.84% in 1995, a decline of 35%.

All the categories in Table 20 showed an increase in terms of aggregate giving in both current and inflation-adjusted dollars. However, giving as a percentage of income provides additional information. Per capita giving as a portion of income to education decreased 13% during this period, health decreased 29%, and giving to human services declined 41%.

Figure 14 presents two views of five use categories: education; health; human services; arts, culture, and humanities; and public/society benefit. The view in the left column presents the aggregate AAFRC data in both current and inflation-adjusted 1996 dollars. This is the view presented in the *Giving USA* series for each use category. The view in the right column for each use category presents the AAFRC data on a per capita basis as a percentage of U.S. per capita disposable personal income.

The decline to human services as a portion of per capita disposable personal income is an important indicator. Often, when the trends in religious giving discussed in other chapters of this report are presented, a frequent question from the listeners is whether individuals have withdrawn giving from their churches and directed it to other helping agencies. Since giving to religion declined by 8%, using the AAFRC published series, or 35%, using the revised denomination-based series, while per capita giving to human services declined by 41% as a portion of income, the data does not support a withdrawal from religious giving in favor of specialized human service agencies.

The two use categories that show an increase are arts, culture and humanities, and the category of public/society benefit. While neither group represented more than 0.2% of per capita giving as a portion of income in 1995, both posted increases between 1968 and 1995, in contrast to the other categories in the table.

The Need for Data Sources for the AAFRC Estimate of Giving. A detailed presentation of the data from which AAFRC prepares the *Giving USA* series would be helpful to both researchers and journalists in their attempts to inform the general public. There are nine sectors plus the category of "Undesignated" included in *Giving USA*. It is difficult to evaluate AAFRC's data over time without information, in tabular form, such as: the source (individual, corporate, foundation, bequest) of contributions to a given use category; the amount from that source; the numerical data which served as a basis for the source estimate within each use category, in adequate detail. AAFRC does not currently publish this data in its *Giving USA* series.

Estimates of Total Individual Charitable Giving in the United States. In addition to the AAFRC *Giving USA* series, the other major source of charitable giving patterns is the Independent Sector *Giving and Volunteering in America* series.

The year 1995 is the last year for which comparable data is available for both AAFRC and Independent Sector estimates of philanthropy. As cited above, the AAFRC estimate of individual dollars contributed to charity in 1995 was $112.2 billion.

The Independent Sector estimate is derived from surveys which Independent Sector commissioned the Gallup Organization to conduct. The results were then analyzed by Independent Sector's research staff, and published in a series of reports titled *Giving and Volunteering*. According to the most recent report, "In 1995, the average household contribution for all respondents (including noncontributors) was $696 . . . "[40]

AAFRC used the category of U.S. personal income to consider its individual giving as a percent of income. Independent Sector used its own survey-based estimate of household

---

[40] Virginia Hodgkinson and Murray S. Weitzman, ed., *Giving and Volunteering in the United States 1996* (Washington, DC: Independent Sector, 1996), 19.

Figure 14:   AAFRC Use Category Data, 1968-1995

Giving to Education

Aggregate

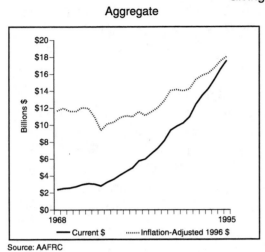

Source: AAFRC

Per Capita

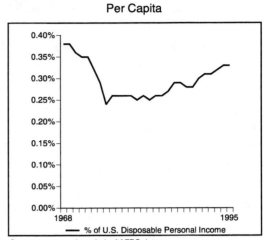

Source: empty tomb analysis, AAFRC data

Giving to Health

Aggregate

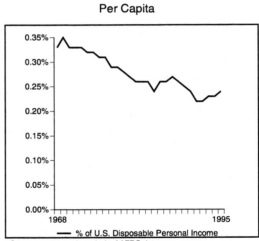

Source: AAFRC

Per Capita

Source: empty tomb analysis, AAFRC data

Giving to Human Services

Aggregate

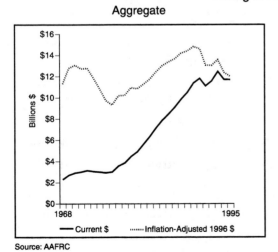

Source: AAFRC

Per Capita

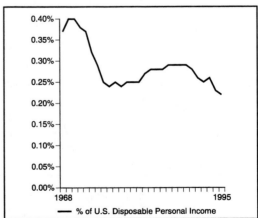

Source: empty tomb analysis, AAFRC data

Figure 14:   AAFRC Use Category Data, 1968-1995, Cont.

Giving to Arts, Culture, and Humanities

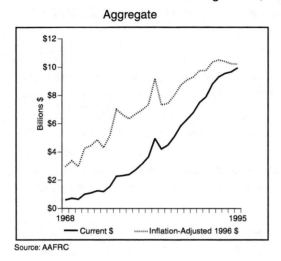

Aggregate

Source: AAFRC

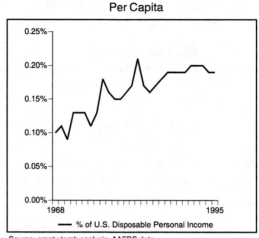

Per Capita

Source: empty tomb analysis, AAFRC data

Giving to Public/Society Benefit

Aggregate

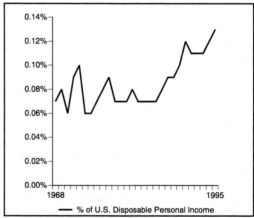

Per Capita

Source: AAFRC

Source: empty tomb analysis, AAFRC data

income to convert its household giving to a percent of income. Nevertheless, *Giving USA 1997* notes, "The average household surveyed by Independent Sector, including those that did not give at all, reported 1995 contributions equal to 1.7% of annual household income, the same as in 1993. *Giving USA* estimates the average percentage of household income contributed from all households in 1995 at 1.9%."[41] A chart on page 64 of *Giving USA* refers to individual, rather than household giving. Even so, the comparison may suggest to the reader that the findings between the two groups were comparable.

Further, the Independent Sector report notes, "Special attention is given to demographics in this survey as it was in the 1992, 1990 and 1988 surveys. Therefore, oversamples of blacks, persons of Hispanic origin and affluent households were included in this study to trace the level of participation by these various groups in the traditions of giving

---

[41] Kaplan, *Giving USA 1997*, 63.

and voluntary service."[42] The methodology notes, "Weighting procedures were used to ensure that the final sample was representative of the adult population in the United States in terms of age, education, marital status, occupation, size of household, region of the country and household income."[43]

AAFRC presents its data for various estimates of giving—individual, corporate, foundation and bequests—in terms of aggregate amounts. Independent Sector presents its data in terms of average household contributions. In order for the Independent Sector household data to be compared with the AAFRC estimate of total individual giving for purposes of the present study, the Independent Sector figure was multiplied by the number of households in the U.S. in the same year for which a charitable contribution figure was obtained to produce an aggregate figure for the Independent Sector survey on total giving by Americans. The resulting aggregated Independent Sector figure is $69.3 billion, representing total giving by Americans in 1995.

The Independent Sector and AAFRC estimates of total individual philanthropy for 1995 differ by $42.9 billion, on a possible base ranging from $69 billion to $112 billion.

Previous editions in *The State of Church Giving* series have compared the AAFRC and Independent Sector estimates of giving in some detail.[44] The present discussion updates the information with 1995 data.

As noted in Table 21, the aggregated Independent Sector estimates for total individual charitable giving were $51.2 billion in 1987, $68.5 billion in 1989, $62.1 billion in 1991, $62.7 billion in 1993, and $69.3 billion in 1995.

AAFRC estimated that total individual charitable giving was $72.3 billion in 1987, $87.8 billion in 1989, $96.1 billion in 1991, $102.1 billion in 1993, and $112.2 billion in 1995.[45]

Thus, the difference between these two estimates varied from $21.1 billion in 1987 to $42.9 billion in 1995.

Figure 15 presents the total individual charitable giving data for Independent Sector's *Giving and Volunteering* and AAFRC's *Giving USA* in graphic form.

The variation in estimates, both in trends and amounts, of individual giving can also be seen when the aggregate data for Independent Sector and AAFRC are converted to per capita giving. A per capita figure was obtained by dividing each aggregate number by the

---

[42] Hodgkinson and Weitzman, 1996, xiii.

[43] Hodgkinson and Weitzman, 1996, xiv. The sentence immediately preceding the weighting explanation reads, "The sampling procedure did not target the very wealthy (those with incomes above $200,000) because they constitute such a small percentage of the population."

[44] John Ronsvalle and Sylvia Ronsvalle, *The State of Church Giving through 1989* (Champaign, IL: empty tomb, inc., 1991), 18-36, *The State of Church Giving through 1991* (1993), 33-57, and *The State of Church Giving through 1993* (1995), 41-58.

[45] Kaplan, *Giving USA 1997*, 198.

Table 21:   Individual Giving, Independent Sector[46] and AAFRC, 1987, 1989, 1991, 1993, and 1995, Aggregate Current Dollars and Percent Change

Year	Independent Sector		AAFRC		Difference Between Independent Sector and AAFRC Estimates (Billions $)	Difference as Percent from Independent Sector Base
	Individual Giving (Billions $)	% Change from Previous Base	Individual Giving (Billions $)	% Change from Previous Base		
1987	$51.2		$72.3		$21.1	41%
1989	$68.5	34%	$87.8	21%	$19.3	28%
1991	$62.1	-9%	$96.1	10%	$34.0	55%
1993	$62.7	1%	$102.1	6%	$39.4	63%
1995	$69.3	11%	$112.2	10%	$42.9	62%

Details in the above table may not compute to the numbers shown due to rounding.

U.S. population[47] for the same year as the charitable giving estimate. The U.S. population, as well as current dollar and inflation-adjusted dollar per capita data, are listed in Table 23 below. Since the Independent Sector analysis uses the Consumer Price Index (CPI) and converts current dollars to what Independent Sector refers to as constant 1995 dollars, that deflator keyed to 1995 was used as noted in the following analyses.

---

[46] Hodgkinson and Weitzman, ed., *Giving and Volunteering 1996*, 20. The household contribution data was multiplied by the number of households for the respective year to obtain aggregate data, as presented in Table 22. The source for the number of households in the United States is as follows: U.S. Bureau of the Census, Current Population reports, Series P-60: 1987, 1989: No. 182RD, *Measuring the Effect of Benefits and Taxes on Income and Poverty: 1979 to 1991* (Washington, DC: U.S. Government Printing Office, 1992), 1; 1991: No. 180, *Money Income of Households, Families and Persons in the United States* (Washington, DC: U.S. Government Printing Office, August 1992), 5; 1993: No. 188, *Income, Poverty, and Valuation of Noncash Benefits: 1993* (Washington, DC: U.S. Government Printing Office, 1995), 5; 1995, No. 193, *Money Income in the United States: 1995 (With Separate Data on Valuation of Noncash Benefits)*, U.S. Government Printing Office, Washington, DC, 1996, 5.

Table 22:   Independent Sector Per Household Contribution Aggregated by Number of Households in the United States, 1987, 1989, 1991, 1993, and 1995, Current Dollars

Year	Independent Sector Household Contribution	Number of Households in the United States	Aggregate of Independent Sector Household Contributions (billions of $)
1987	$562	91,124,000	$51.2
1989	$734	93,347,000	$68.5
1991	$649	95,669,000	$62.1
1993	$646	97,107,000	$62.7
1995	$696	99,627,000	$69.3

Details in the above table may not compute to the numbers shown due to rounding.

[47] The sources for U.S. population is as follows: 1987: U.S. Department of Commerce Bureau of Economic Analysis *National Income and Product Accounts of the United States: Volume 2, 1959-1988* (Washington, DC: U.S. Government Printing Office, September 1992), Table 8.2, 330; 1989: *Survey of Current Business*, Table 8.2, December 1991, 16; 1991 and 1993: *Survey of Current Business*, July 1994, 111; 1995: *Survey of Current Business*, May 1997, D-25

Figure 15:   Individual Giving, Independent Sector and AAFRC, 1987, 1989, 1991, 1993 and 1995, Aggregate Current Dollars

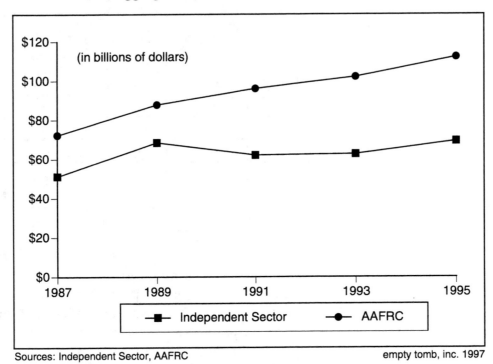

Sources: Independent Sector, AAFRC   empty tomb, inc. 1997

Table 23:   Individual Giving, Independent Sector and AAFRC, 1987, 1989, 1991, 1993, and 1995, Total Current Dollars and Per Capita Current and Constant 1995 Dollars and Percent Change

Year	U.S. Pop. (Millions)	Independent Sector Data				AAFRC *Giving USA* Data			
		Total Individual Charitable Giving, Current $s (Billions)	Per Capita Charitable Giving		% Change from Previous Measure, Per Capita, Constant '95 $	Total Individual Charitable Giving, Current $s (Billions)	Per Capita Charitable Giving		% Change from Previous Measure, Per Capita, Constant '95 $
			Current Dollars	Constant '95 Dollars CPI 82-4=100			Current Dollars	Constant '95 Dollars CPI 82-4=100	
1987	242.9	$51.2	$211	$283		$72.3	$298	$399	
1989	247.4	$68.5	$277	$340	20%	$87.8	$355	$436	9%
1991	252.7	$62.1	$246	$275	-19%	$96.1	$380	$426	-2%
1993	258.3	$62.7	$243	$256	-7%	$102.1	$395	$417	-2%
1995	263.1	$69.3	$264	$264	3%	$112.2	$427	$427	2%

Details in the above table may not compute to the numbers shown due to rounding.

Figure 16 presents the percent change in per capita individual charitable contributions from 1987 to 1995, from the 1987 base, in graphic form.

The Independent Sector data suggests some volatility in individual giving to charity from 1987 to 1995. The AAFRC data suggests a steady increase in current dollars, and an increase followed by a decline followed by an increase in constant dollars.

For the researcher, the news reporter, or the concerned citizen, it is difficult to obtain a clear picture of individual philanthropy in the United States, given the differences between these two information sources. *Giving USA 1996* notes, "Researchers frequently agree on the

Figure 16: **Individual Charitable Contributions, Independent Sector and AAFRC, 1987-1995, Per Capita Constant 1995 Dollars, Percent Change from 1987 Base**

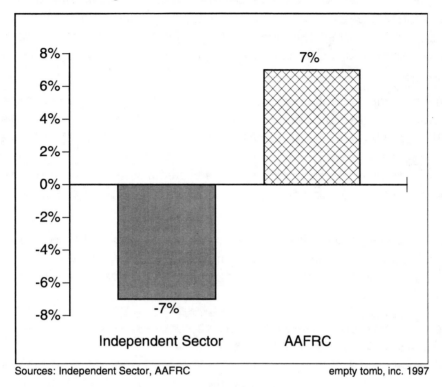

Sources: Independent Sector, AAFRC   empty tomb, inc. 1997

direction of total giving and the general magnitude of that trend."[48] While, to their credit, both Independent Sector and AAFRC indicate that they are regularly working to improve their estimates of giving, the data in Table 23 would suggest more refinement is needed.

Estimates of Giving to Religion. Both Independent Sector and AAFRC also provide estimates of giving to religion.

The Independent Sector estimate is for household contributions to religion. In accordance with the above consideration of total contributions by individuals, the estimate of giving to religion was aggregated by multiplying the household contribution by the number of households in the United States.

The AAFRC estimate is for religious giving from all sources, including individual, corporation, bequest and foundation, with, as noted before, AAFRC suggesting "most giving to religion" coming from individuals. Without the additional information from AAFRC as to how much money came from each source of contribution to their use category of religion, the following comparison uses the entire religion figure as AAFRC's estimate of giving to religion for individuals.

A third source of information on giving to religion is from a set of 28 Protestant denominations which published data in the *Yearbook of American and Canadian Churches*

---

[48] Kaplan, *Giving USA 1996*, 195.

(*YACC*) series for the years 1987, 1989, 1991, 1993 and 1995.[49] Inasmuch as these communions include 40 million full or confirmed members, they represent a sizable portion of the church in the United States. This data is based on actual reports from more than 100,000 of the estimated 350,000 religious congregations of any type in the United States. So while the data does not provide a complete picture of religious giving, the percentage change from year to year provides important information about changes in religious giving for purposes of comparison.

The Independent Sector data suggested a 30% increase in aggregated current dollar giving to religion from 1987 to 1989, a 12% decrease from 1989 to 1991, essentially no change from 1991 to 1993, and a 6% increase from 1993 to 1995. Both the AAFRC data and *YACC* reports suggest that giving to religion increased in each set of two years in the period 1987 to 1995. However, while the *YACC* reports indicated that the rate of increase in each two-year set varied between 6% and 10%, the increases in the AAFRC estimate varied from 4% to 18%.

Table 24 compares the levels of aggregate religious giving for Independent Sector, AAFRC, and the set of 28 denominations publishing data in the *Yearbook of American and Canadian Churches*, as well as the percent change from year to year for each.

Table 24: **Giving to Religion, Independent Sector, AAFRC, and 28 *YACC* Denominations, 1987, 1989, 1991, 1993 and 1995, Aggregate Current Dollars and Percent Change**

Year	Independent Sector		AAFRC		*YACC* Set of 28 Denominations	
	Giving to Religion (Billions $)	Percent Change from Previous Base	Giving to Religion (Billions $)	Percent Change from Previous Base	Giving to Religion (Billions $)	Percent Change from Previous Base
1987	$34.2		$43.5		$14.6	
1989	$44.5	30%	$47.8	10%	$16.0	10%
1991	$39.2	-12%	$53.9	13%	$17.4	8%
1993	$39.0	0%	$56.3	4%	$18.5	6%
1995	$41.5	6%	$66.3	18%	$20.2	9%

Details in the above table may not compute to the numbers shown due to rounding.

As noted earlier, *Giving USA 1997* noted that the Independent Sector estimate of household contributions to charity was 1.7% of income in 1995 while the AAFRC estimate of individual giving was 1.9%. There is a 12% difference between those estimates of two different categories from the Independent Sector base.

Yet comparing aggregate estimates of 1995 giving to religion, Independent Sector's data yields an estimate of $41.5 billion while the AAFRC figure is $66.3 billion. The AAFRC estimate is 60% greater than the Independent Sector estimate.

---

[49] This group of 28 denominations includes 26 of the 29 denominations in the 1968-1995 analysis in chapter one. These 26 denominations reported data for the five years under consideration. The Episcopal Church and The United Methodist Church are also included in the set of 28 denominations.

Table 25 presents per capita data, in both current and constant dollars, for Independent Sector and AAFRC estimates of giving to religion.

Table 25: **Giving to Religion, Independent Sector and AAFRC, 1987, 1989, 1991, 1993 and 1995, Aggregate Current and Per Capita Current and Constant 1995 Dollars and Percent Change**

Year	U.S. Pop. (Millions)	Independent Sector Data				AAFRC *Giving USA* Data			
		Religious Giving, Current $s (Billions)	Per Capita Religious Giving		% Change from Previous Measure, Per Capita, Constant '95$s	Religious Giving, Current $s (Billions)	Per Capita Religious Giving		% Change from Previous Measure, Per Capita, Constant '95$s
			Current Dollars	Constant '95 Dollars CPI 82-4=100			Current Dollars	Constant '95 Dollars CPI 82-4=100	
1987	242.9	$34.2	$141	$189		$43.5	$179	$240	
1989	247.4	$44.5	$180	$221	17%	$47.8	$193	$237	-1%
1991	252.7	$39.2	$155	$174	-21%	$53.9	$213	$239	1%
1993	258.3	$39.0	$151	$159	-8%	$56.3	$218	$230	-4%
1995	263.1	$41.5	$158	$158	-1%	$66.3	$252	$252	10%

Details in the above table may not compute to the numbers shown due to rounding.

Figure 17 presents a comparison of Independent Sector and AAFRC data for giving to religion in graphic form.

Figure 17: **Giving to Religion, Independent Sector and AAFRC, 1987, 1989, 1991, 1993 and 1995, Aggregate Current Dollars**

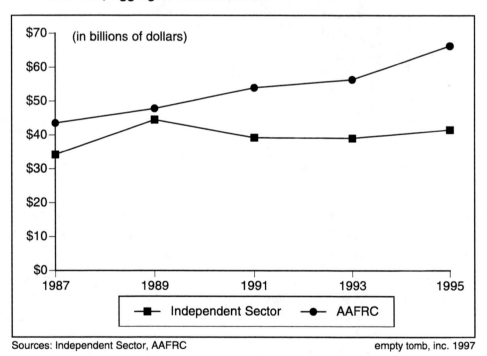

Sources: Independent Sector, AAFRC   empty tomb, inc. 1997

The estimates from the two sources of charitable giving information vary in both amount, and in trend lines. The result can be a confused picture about the practice of philanthropy in the United States, especially if those relying on the data are not aware of the variation that exists in the estimates of how much Americans give.

A Comparison of Estimates of Giving to Religion. A final comparison can be made between three sources of giving to religion. Earlier in this chapter, a comparison was made of the AAFRC giving to religion with a revised denomination-based series keyed to the Filer Commission 1974 estimate of giving to religion. The figures for Independent Sector's estimate of giving to religion can be compared to these other two estimates.

The AAFRC 1995 figure for giving to religion was $66.3 billion. The revised denomination-based series estimated that giving to religion in 1995 was $44.5 billion. The Independent Sector figure for giving to religion was $41.5 billion. Figure 18 presents this data in graphic form.

Figure 18:   Giving to Religion, AAFRC, Denomination-Based Series Keyed to the Filer Commission Estimate, and Independent Sector, 1995

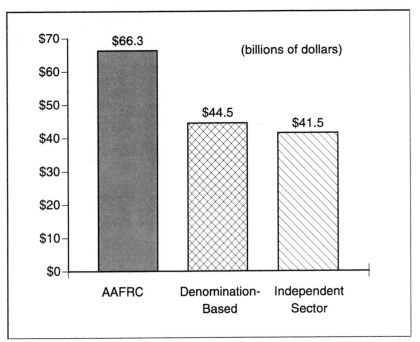

Sources: AAFRC; Denomination-based series   empty tomb, inc. 1997
Independent Sector

External Validation of Data. Previous editions in the *State of Church Giving* series discuss the importance of external validation of survey data. What follows is an update of validation trials conducted on Independent Sector data, based on additional 1995 data.

The following comparisons are illustrations of validation trials applied to four areas of Independent Sector's findings in *Giving and Volunteering 1996*. These comparisons highlight both the approach that might be taken to validate the instrument for future surveys, as well as the need for such validation. Again, in keeping with Independent Sector methodology, the Consumer Price Index was used to convert current dollars to constant 1995 dollars.

Income Validation Trial. Independent Sector employs surveys to estimate U.S. household income and household charitable contributions. These two data streams are combined to produce an estimate of giving as a percentage of income.

Table 26 compares Independent Sector survey household income in current and constant dollars[50] with U.S. Census Bureau household income.[51] The Consumer Price Index was used to convert the Census Bureau current dollar household income to constant 1995 dollars as well. This comparison provides important information about the Independent Sector data because it uses 100% of the universe of Independent Sector respondents. As the editors of the *Giving and Volunteering* series note, "The reader is cautioned to view the numbers in this report as patterns or trends. While the error rate for the whole sample population is plus or minus 3 percent, the error rate could be much larger for small portions of the sample, particularly when only a small percentage of respondents report giving and volunteering to a certain area."[52] In the case of income, however, the entire sample size in the survey is included.

Both the U.S. Census Bureau and the Independent Sector current dollar household income figures increased between 1987 and 1995. When converted to constant 1995 dollars, the Census Bureau household income data posted an increase from 1987 to 1989, a decrease from 1989 to 1991, an increase from 1991 to 1993, and again from 1993 to 1995. The Independent Sector household income data indicated a different trend, with a decrease for every two-year period between 1987 and 1993, and an increase from 1993 to 1995. At a number of key points, the Independent Sector survey household data differs both in amount and in the direction of trends from the U.S. Census Bureau data.

Table 26 summarizes this household income data comparison.

Table 26: Household Income Validation Trial, Independent Sector and U.S. Census Household Income, 1987, 1989, 1991, 1993 and 1995, Current Dollars, Constant 1995 Dollars and Percent Change

Year	Independent Sector Household Income Estimate			U.S. Census Bureau Household Income Data		
	Current Dollars	Constant '95 Dollars CPI 82-4=100	% Change in Constant $, from previous base	Current Dollars	Constant '95 Dollars CPI 82-4=100	% Change in Constant $, from previous base
1987	$34,498	$46,281		$32,410	$43,480	
1989	$35,972	$44,211	-4%	$36,520	$44,884	3%
1991	$36,797	$41,174	-7%	$37,922	$42,433	-5%
1993	$37,493	$39,543	-4%	$41,428	$43,693	3%
1995	$41,484	$41,484	5%	$44,938	$44,938	3%

Details in the above table may not compute to the numbers shown due to rounding.

Figure 19 presents a comparison of Independent Sector and U.S. Census Bureau household income data in graphic form.

---

[50] Hodgkinson and Weitzman, *Giving and Volunteering, 1996*, 20.

[51] U.S. Census Bureau Current Dollar household income: Current Population Reports, Series P-60: 1987-91: No. 182-RD, August 1992, p. 1; 1993: No. 188, February 1995, p. 5; 1995: No. 193, p. 5.

[52] Hodgkinson and Weitzman, *Giving and Volunteering, 1996*, xiv.

Figure 19: **Household Income, Independent Sector and U.S. Census Bureau, 1987, 1989, 1991, 1993 and 1995, Constant 1995 Dollars**

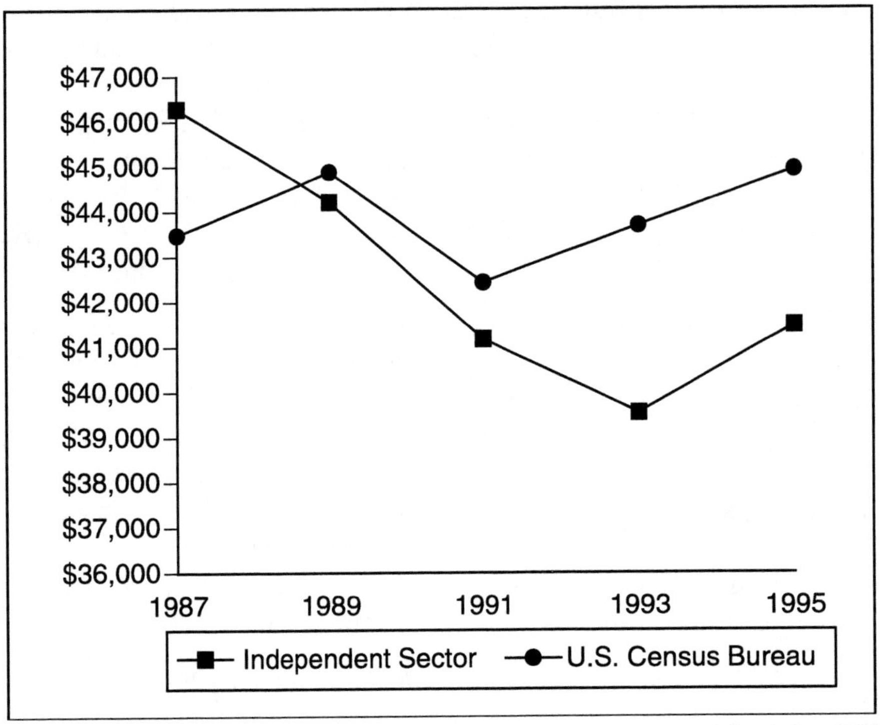

Sources: Independent Sector, U.S. Census Bureau   empty tomb, inc. 1997

Education Validation Trial. Table 27 below presents data on giving to Education. Independent Sector per capita data was obtained as follows. The Independent Sector current dollar household contribution to Education[53] was multiplied by the number of households in the United States for the appropriate year. The resulting aggregate was then divided by U.S. population for the appropriate year to yield a per capita figure. The Consumer Price Index was used to convert the resulting per capita figure to constant 1995 dollars.

The aggregate Council for Aid to Education data for the categories of Higher Education from the Alumni and Others categories was combined to produce a Higher Education Contribution from Individuals figure.[54] This combined Individuals figure was then divided by the U.S. population figures noted above, to produce a per capita Higher Education contribution figure. In the fiscal year ending in 1995, Higher Education contributions from individuals were estimated to represent 51% of the gifts to Higher Education.[55]

---

[53] Hodgkinson and Weitzman, *Giving and Volunteering, 1994, Volume I*, 19, and *Giving and Volunteering 1996*, 25.

[54] Data years 1987, 1989 and 1991 are based on data presented in *Voluntary Support of Education 1992* (New York: Council for Aid to Education, 1992), 43. Data years 1993 and 1995 are based on data presented in David R. Morgan, *1996 Voluntary Support of Education* (New York: Council for Aid to Education, 1997), 42. For a description of the process that converted academic year data to calendar year data, see the footnote to Table 27 below.

[55] Morgan, *1996 Voluntary Support of Education*, 3.

The Council for Aid to Education data for individual contributions includes gifts from bequests as well as living donors. The Council for Aid to Education, in a table titled "Bequests and Deferred Gifts, 1977-1996" lists data for individual gifts, bequests and deferred gifts. In fiscal year 1995-1996, the portion of contributions from bequests represented 24.2% of all gifts and deferred gifts represented 15.1%.[56] The following comparison, therefore, only suggests the type of trial which could be undertaken to validate the Independent Sector survey results after the Council for Aid to Education individual giving amounts were adjusted as necessary for bequest and deferred giving data.

The Independent Sector per capita contribution to Education posted a 17% increase in constant 1995 dollars from 1987 to 1989, a 23% decrease from 1989 to 1991, a 47% increase from 1991 to 1993, and a 16% decrease from 1993 to 1995. The Council on Aid to Education data for Higher Education decreased by 2% in constant 1995 dollars from 1987 to 1989, stayed about the same from 1989 to 1991, increased by 5% from 1991 to 1993, and increased 11% from 1993 to 1995. Table 27 summarizes the comparison data on contributions to Education.

Table 27: **Education Validation Trial, Independent Sector Giving to Education and Council for Aid to Education Contributions to Higher Education, 1987, 1989, 1991, 1993 and 1995, Aggregate Current Dollars, Per Capita Current Dollars, Constant 1995 Dollars and Percent Change** [57]

	Independent Sector Contribution to Education Estimate				Council for Aid to Education Contribution to Higher Education Adjusted Estimate			
			Per Capita				Per Capita	
Calendar Year	Total Contributions Current $ (Billions)	Current Dollars	Constant '95 Dollars CPI 82-4=100	% Change in Constant $, from Previous Base	Total Contributions Current $ (Billions)	Current Dollars	Constant '95 Dollars CPI 82-4=100	% Change in Constant $, from Previous Base
1987	$4.0	$17	$22		$4.2	$17	$23	
1989	$5.2	$21	$26	17%	$4.6	$18	$23	-2%
1991	$4.5	$18	$20	-23%	$5.1	$20	$23	0%
1993	$7.2	$28	$29	47%	$5.9	$23	$24	5%
1995	$6.5	$25	$25	-16%	$7.0	$27	$27	11%

Details in the above table may not compute to the numbers shown due to rounding.

---

[56] *Voluntary Support of Education, 1996*, 17.

[57] The Council for Aid to Education Voluntary Support for Higher Education from Individuals data (VSE) was converted from a July 1 through June 30 fiscal year to a calendar year, as follows. The VSE data was converted from its reported fiscal year form to a calendar year form by dividing the fiscal year VSE data into two parts which were proportionate to four quarters of U.S. BEA average annual per capita disposable personal income which had been compiled to parallel the VSE data's fiscal year. For example, the sum of the average annual income for Q1 and Q2 for 1981 comprised 51.3% of the total of average income for those two quarters plus the average annual income for Q3 and Q4 of 1980. The 1981 Q1 and Q2's 51.3% of the $2.056 billion VSE data for FY 1980-81 was $1.054 billion. Repeating this process for FY 1981-82 yielded a second half year's VSE data for calendar year 1981. This process was repeated for FYs 1980-81 through 1995-96 yielding calendar year data for the years 1981 through 1995. The Calendar Year (FY Changed for Inflation and Growth in the Economy) VSE data is compared to the Independent Sector Education data in Table 27 in the main body text above. For a more detailed discussion of the conversion method used, see Ronsvalle and Ronsvalle, *The State of Church Giving through 1991*, p. 48, footnote 50.

Figure 20 presents per capita contributions data for Independent Sector and Council for Aid to Education in graphic form.

Figure 20: **Giving to Education, Independent Sector and Council for Aid to Education, 1987, 1989, 1991, 1993 and 1995, Per Capita Constant 1995 Dollars**

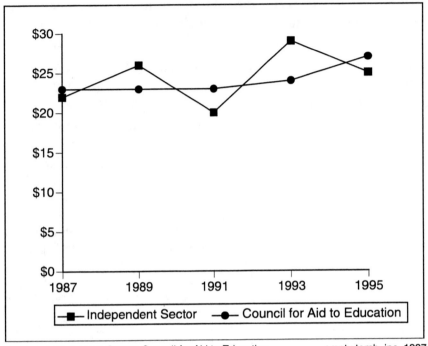

Sources: Independent Sector, Council for Aid to Education   empty tomb, inc. 1997

The trend lines also produce overall variable results. The 1987 to 1993 data in per capita constant dollars indicated that Independent Sector giving to education increased by 32% while the Council for Aid to Education increased by 3%. However, when the data set was extended to include 1995, the Independent Sector data had increased by 11% from 1987 compared to the Council for Aid to Education data increasing by 15%. Figure 21 presents the 1987-1995 percent change in per capita constant dollar contributions to education for both Independent Sector and the Council for Aid to Education in graphic form.

Methodists Validation Trial. Table 28 presents data for giving by Methodists. As noted earlier, Independent Sector indicates that "the error rate could be much larger for small portions of the sample, particularly when only a small percentage of respondents report giving and volunteering to a certain area."[58] However, the data published in the *Giving and Volunteering* series may still be used and quoted by practitioners and others in spite of that caveat. Were Independent Sector's sample for specific large denominations such that the error rate were within acceptable limits, it would be possible to conduct validation trials of its survey instrument. Table 28 compares Independent Sector findings for Methodists with the largest Methodist denomination in the U.S., The United Methodist Church, which is the

---

[58] Hodgkinson and Weitzman, *Giving and Volunteering in the United States 1996*, xix.

Figure 21: **Giving to Education, Independent Sector and Council for Aid to Education, 1987-1995, Per Capita Constant 1995 Dollars, Percent Change from 1987 Base**

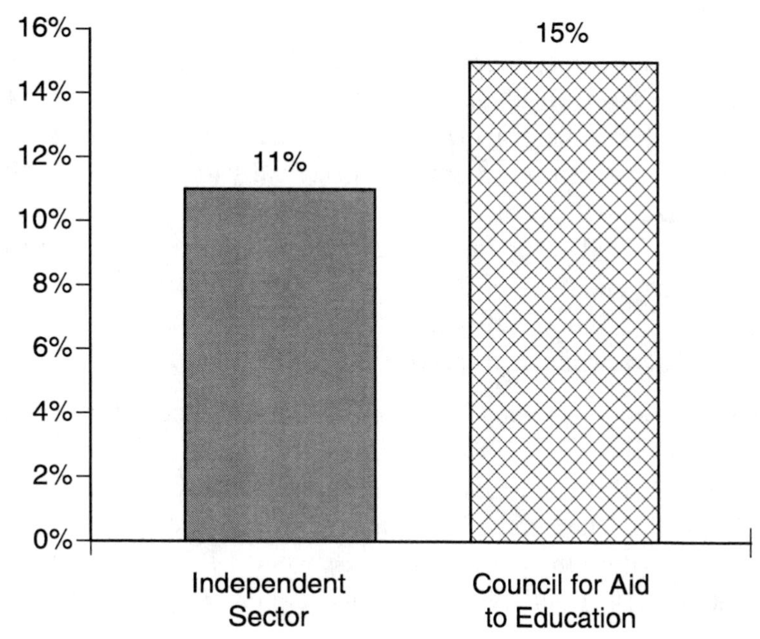

Sources: Independent Sector, Council for Aid to Education   empty tomb, inc. 1997

second largest Protestant communion, and which represented 3.24% of the U.S. population in 1995. This denomination is an example of one of the five or so large denominations which could each be used in a validation trial.

The Independent Sector Methodist data in Table 28 was derived as follows. The Independent Sector estimate for the percentage of Methodist respondents was multiplied by the number of households in the United States for the appropriate year. The resulting number of Methodist households was multiplied by the current dollar household contribution by Methodists, to yield a Total Contributions by Methodist households figure. The U.S. population for the relevant year was multiplied by the percentage of Methodist respondents in the Independent Sector survey to yield a Methodist population figure. The aggregated Total Contributions by Methodist households figure was then divided by the Methodist population figure to produce a per capita Methodist figure.[59]

A review of the constant dollar data yielded the following patterns. The Independent Sector per Methodist data suggested an increased contribution from 1987 to 1989, a decrease

---

[59] The Independent Sector data is from the following editions of Hodgkinson and Weitzman, *Giving and Volunteering*: 1987 data, 1988 edition, page 17, (Methodist percent of population of 9.1% from correspondence dated 9/29/93 from Heather A. Gorski, Research Associate of Independent Sector); 1989 data, 1990 edition, page 60; 1991 data, 1992 edition, page 76; 1993 data, 1994 edition, Volume I, page 115; 1995 data, 1996 edition, page 152. The United Methodist Church membership and financial data is from the relevant edition of the *Yearbook of American and Canadian Churches* (Nashville, TN: Abingdon Press).

from 1989 to 1991, an increase from 1991 to 1993, and a decrease from 1993 to 1995. The United Methodist Church per full or confirmed member data posted an increase from 1987 to 1989, essentially no change from 1989 to 1991, an increase from 1991 to 1993, and again from 1993 to 1995.

The Independent Sector data measured the equivalent of inclusive membership contributions to the church, as well as any contributions made by Methodists to other religious and nonreligious charitable organizations. The United Methodist data measured largely contributions of full or confirmed members specifically to the congregation. Such a distinction highlights the fact that, were the proposed Independent Sector validation trial question framed so that it asked respondents for the amount contributed to their local congregation in one question, and to other philanthropy categories in a separate question, a sharper comparison could be made between Independent Sector survey findings and published denominational data which summarizes congregational giving.

In this trial, the Independent Sector findings that Methodist per capita constant dollar contributions increased 64% between 1987 and 1989, decreased 31% between 1989 and 1991, increased 3% between 1991 and 1993, and decreased 25% between 1993 and 1995, need to be reviewed in light of The United Methodist Church reports indicating that full or confirmed per member contributions increased 3% between 1987 and 1989, 0% between 1989 and 1991, 2% between 1991 and 1993, and 4% between 1993 and 1995.

Table 28:   **Methodists Validation Trial, Independent Sector Methodist Data and Data for The United Methodist Church, 1987, 1989, 1991, 1993 and 1995, Aggregate Current Dollars, Per Capita Current Dollars, Constant 1995 Dollars and Percent Change**

| Year | Independent Sector Methodist Contributions to All Causes | | | | Contributions to The United Methodist Church Congregations | | | |
| | | Per Capita | | | | Per Full/Confirmed Member | | |
	Total Current Dollars (Billions)	Current Dollars	Constant '95 Dollars CPI 82-4=100	% Change in Constant $, from Previous Base	Total Current Dollars (Billions)	Current Dollars	Constant '95 Dollars CPI 82-4=100	% Change in Constant $, from Previous Base
1987	$3.8	$173	$233		$2.6	$284	$381	
1989	$7.4	$310	$381	64%	$2.8	$320	$393	3%
1991	$5.7	$235	$264	-31%	$3.1	$353	$395	0%
1993	$6.4	$258	$272	3%	$3.3	$382	$403	2%
1995	$4.1	$203	$203	-25%	$3.6	$418	$418	4%

Details in the above table may not compute to the numbers shown due to rounding.

Observations about the Validation Trials. The three comparisons of income, education, and Methodist giving yield substantial variation between the trends provided by the Independent Sector data and three sets of external validation data. These differences would suggest that some refinement in the survey tool may be necessary to produce a more reliable information resource about the charitable donation habits evidenced by Americans, including church members. It would be helpful if the *Giving and Volunteering* series would list the plus and minus percentage range for the error rate for each category and subcategory for which they provide data, so that those members of the general public using the data would readily be able to gauge the applicability of the findings.

Another area of Independent Sector research which would benefit from such validation trials would be the *From Belief to Commitment* series which is published every five years. These reports consider congregation-level expenditures. Such validation could be accomplished by sampling, and reporting, a sufficient number of congregations for a select group of denominations which regularly publish fairly extensive financial data in the *Yearbook of American and Canadian Churches* series.

Summary. There are two major sources of total charitable giving information in the United States.

The American Association of Fund-Raising Counsel, Inc. (AAFRC) publishes the *Giving USA* series. AAFRC actually produces two estimates of giving for the most recent year. One is a projection based on an econocentric model to produce an estimate for individual contributions. This individual giving projection is combined with estimates for bequests, foundations and corporations to produce a total charitable giving estimate by source of contribution. A second estimate of giving for the most recent year is defined by use of contribution, including surveys within some use categories. Any discrepancy between the two totals has, in the past, been assigned to either religion or another use category, such as "undesignated" or "unclassified."

Since AAFRC revises its past data, notably individual giving, as additional information becomes available, this revised series comprises a third estimate within the *Giving USA* series.

When a 1968-1995 denomination-based series keyed to the Filer Commission 1974 estimate of giving to religion was compared to the AAFRC series, the 1995 AAFRC estimate for giving to religion of $66.26 billion was 49% higher than the denomination-based series estimate of $44.5 billion. This same difference was therefore reflected when the same denomination-based series was used to revise the AAFRC total charitable giving estimate series and the individual giving series.

The AAFRC data was also considered on a per capita basis, to account for population changes, and as a portion of U.S. per capita disposable personal income, to account for the changes in taxes during the 1968-1995 period.

The AAFRC estimates were also higher than the other source of total individual giving information, the Independent Sector *Giving and Volunteering in the United States* series. These two sources differed by $42.9 billion in their estimates of 1995 individual charitable giving, on a base that ranged from the Independent Sector estimate of $69 billion to the AAFRC estimate of $112 billion.

A series of validation tests on the Independent Sector data found that the Independent Sector data was more volatile than three external sources of comparable data.

7

The Theological Implications of Church Member Giving Patterns_____

"Why do you call me 'Lord, Lord,' and do not do what I say"?

— Jesus Christ, quoted in Luke 6:46 (NIV)

Grace has symptoms. If one does not have the symptoms, does one have the condition?

This question may be controversial in light of centuries of debate. The general topic is often summarized as "grace/law" or "faith/works." Yet, the continuing decline evident in church member giving data, as reviewed in earlier chapters of this report, calls for a consideration of the theological implications of these patterns.

Various aspects of the demographic and sociological implications of the data have been discussed in previous editions in this series.[60] However, as these patterns describe the behavior of the members of religious congregations, the theological implications ought also to be discussed.

Further, the important, and often intense, debates about the relationship between salvation, faith and works, and the role of grace and law, may not be the defining topics in the present discussion. Rather, a more basic issue needs attention, an issue that might be summarized as "faith/no faith." An overview of the issues involved in the present discussion may be framed by the question, Can giving patterns provide any indication about whether church members have faith? Further, the implications of not having faith can be considered.

---

[60] See, for example, "Observations and Reflections" in John Ronsvalle and Sylvia Ronsvalle, *The State of Church Giving (SCG) through 1989* (Champaign, IL: empty tomb, inc., 1991), 37-42; "Church Member Giving in Recession Years"(pages 25-35) and "Church Member Giving and Social Health" (pages 36-45), *SCG through 1990* (1992); "Church Giving in Perspective: Can Church Members Afford to Give More?" in *SCG through 1992* (1994), 43-52; and, "A Unified Theory of Giving and Membership," *SCG through 1993* (1995), 79-97.

Although the issues raised in this chapter deserve a comprehensive treatment, the present discussion will seek only to raise a few key points that may be helpful in suggesting directions for further exploration. First, a brief review of the historical grace/law and faith/works deliberations will consider how the present discussion differs from those topics.

Second, a review of relevant comments from church leaders, including Martin Luther and John Calvin, will consider whether grace, in fact, should have symptoms.

Finally, a brief discussion of church members' responses to historical social challenges may help to put present giving patterns into a broader context.

By Faith Alone. Ecclesiastical practices in the Middle Ages produced a strong reaction among faithful members of the church. Although a variety of behaviors were problematic, the issue that is often used to summarize the recreant conditions at the time is the sale of indulgences.

On October 31, 1517, Martin Luther, an Augustinian monk, reacted to the sale of these special dispensations which, it was promised, could lead to less time in purgatory or to the remission of sin. Luther posted 95 Theses on the Wittenberg Chapel door, in an offer to debate the topics as was standard at the time. Translated from Latin into the vernacular, the Theses found a broad and receptive audience among nobles and commoners alike who were not happy about owing both allegiance and money to Rome. The Protestant Reformation was born.

In fact, such leaders as Francis Xavier and Ignatius Loyola would lead a Catholic Reformation within the structure of the Roman Catholic Church. However, the theological implications most relevant for the present discussion are clearest in the writings of two Protestant Reformation leaders: Martin Luther (1483-1546) and John Calvin (1509-1564).

Luther's 95 Theses describe the objectionable practices of the time. For example, Thesis 27 reads, "There is no divine authority for preaching that the soul flies out of purgatory immediately the money clinks in the bottom of the chest."[61]

Calvin described the practice in the following words:

> But then they have imaginary satisfactions, by means of which those who have sinned purchase back the favour of God. In this class, they place first contrition, and next works, which they term works of supererogation, and penances, which God inflicts on sinners. But, as they are still sensible that these compensations fall far short of the just measure required, they call in the aid of a new species of satisfaction from another quarter, namely, from the benefit of the keys. And they say, that by the keys the treasury of the Church is unlocked, and what is wanting to ourselves supplied out of the merits of Christ and the saints.[62]

In his famous *Institutes*, Calvin comments further: "Now indulgences flow from this doctrine of satisfaction. For our opponents pretend that to make satisfaction those indulgences

---

[61] Martin Luther, *Selections from His Writings*, John Dillenberger, ed. (Garden City, NY: Anchor Books, Doubleday & Company, Inc., 1961), 490.

[62] John Calvin, *Tracts Relating to the Reformation*, Henry Beveridge, trans. (Edinburgh, Scotland: The Calvin Translation Society, 1844), 163.

supply what our powers lack… These men are fit to be treated by drugs for insanity rather than to be argued with." Calvin continues as he describes the spiritual consequences of the practice: "Men saw themselves openly and undisguisedly held up to ridicule… their souls' salvation the object of lucrative trafficking, the price of salvation reckoned at a few coins, nothing offered free of charge."[63]

These leaders felt compelled to develop a more adequate theology, or perhaps more accurately, restate a more faithful theology. For example, in Luther's Thesis 36, he asserts, "Any Christian whatsoever, who is truly repentant, enjoys plenary remission from penalty and guilt, and this is given him without letters of indulgence."[64]

As often happens in the presence of extreme circumstances, Luther and Calvin felt impelled to make as clear as possible the differences between what was actually occurring and what the practices ought to have been. The main theme of many of these writings was justification by faith.

For example, in his *Small Catechism*, Luther explains the third article in the Apostle's Creed as follows:

> Sanctification: I believe in the Holy Ghost; the holy Christian Church, the communion of saints; the forgiveness of sins; the resurrection of the body; and the life everlasting. Amen
>
> *What does this mean?* I believe that I cannot by my own reason or strength believe in Jesus Christ, my Lord, or come to Him; but the Holy Ghost has called me by the Gospel, enlightened me with His gifts, sanctified and kept me in the true faith…[65]

Calvin, too, emphasized the importance of justification by faith. He wrote, "This we call the righteousness of faith, viz., when a man, made void and empty of all confidence in works, feels convinced that the only ground of his acceptance with God is a righteousness which is wanting to himself, and is borrowed from Christ."[66]

This concept became a battle cry of the Protestant Reformation, summed up as *sola fide*, that is, by faith alone.

The concept has been affirmed repeatedly throughout the succeeding centuries. For example, Dietrich Bonhoeffer, Lutheran pastor and German church leader during World War II, writes in *The Cost of Discipleship*:

> The justification of the sinner therefore consists in the sole righteousness of God, wherein the sinner is utterly and completely unrighteous, and has no righteousness whatever of his own, side by side with the righteousness of God. Whenever we desire an independent righteousness of our own we are forfeiting our only chance of justification, which is through God and his righteousness. God alone

---

[63] John Calvin, *Institutes of the Christian Religion*, John T. McNeill, ed. (Philadelphia: Westminster Press, 1960), Vol. II, 670.

[64] Luther, *Selections*, 494.

[65] Martin Luther, *A Short Explanation of Dr. Martin Luther's Small Catechism, A Handbook of Christian Doctrine* (St. Louis, MO: Concordia Publishing House, 1965), 11.

[66] Calvin, *Tracts*, 161.

is righteous. On the cross this truth is apprehended as our condemnation as sinners. But when we are brought to faith in the death of Christ, we receive the righteousness of God...[67]

Ecumenical dialogues continue to affirm this doctrine through the present. The Evangelical Lutheran Church in America is engaged in dialogues with The Episcopal Church, the Reformed Church in America, and the Roman Catholic Church. In all three discussions, the concept of justification by faith is strongly affirmed, as is evidenced in article 3.15 of the Lutheran-Catholic statement: "Together we confess: By grace alone, in faith in Christ's saving work and not because of any merit on our part, we are accepted by God and receive the Holy Spirit, who renews our hearts while equipping and calling us to good works," and again in article 4.1.19: "We confess together that all persons depend completely on the saving grace of God for their salvation."[68]

A less formal dialogue has also been conducted among evangelical and Roman Catholic leaders in the United States. A recent report in *Christianity Today* indicated that leaders from these groups have formulated a statement that reads in part, "We agree that justification is not earned by any good works or merits of our own; it is entirely God's gift, conferred through the Father's sheer graciousness, out of the love that he bears us in his Son, who suffered on our behalf and rose from the dead for our justification."[69]

Acknowledging this basic doctrine of justification by grace, how does this doctrine affect the present discussion of the practice of religion?

Should Grace Have Symptoms? There are a variety of verses throughout the New Testament that call for action on the part of one who would be faithful. How is a church member to understand the relationship between faith and works from within a commitment to the grace of God?

The church has apparently struggled to understand the implications of the present issue since its founding. The apostle Paul, writing in his letter to the Romans, complains that his teaching has been "slanderously reported" by some as encouraging licentiousness in order that God's grace may be more evident (Romans 3:8, NIV).

That moving from the experience of grace to a life consistent with faithfulness was a challenge to the early church may also be inferred from 1 Peter 2:16: "As servants of God, live as free people, yet do not use your freedom as a pretext for evil" (NRSV).

Perhaps a review of some of the verses calling for action, and related comments by Luther and Calvin, may be of assistance.

Matthew 25: 31-46. One of the most familiar passages, and perhaps troubling from within the context of our present discussion, is the parable of the sheep and the goats. In Matthew 25:31-46, Jesus says that when the Son of Man returns, the sheep will be put on his

---

[67] Dietrich Bonhoeffer, *The Cost of Discipleship* (New York: The MacMillan Company, 1963), 308.

[68] Office of the Bishop, Department of Ecumenical Affairs, *Ecumenical Proposals, Documents for Action by the 1997 Churchwide Assembly* (Chicago, IL: Evangelical Lutheran Church in America, 1996), 27.

[69] Evangelicals and Catholics Together, "The Gift of Salvation," *Christianity Today*, December 8, 1997, 36.

right and the goats on the left. The sheep will be welcomed into the kingdom because when they saw the king hungry, thirsty, as a stranger, in need of clothes, sick and in prison, they helped the king. The sheep will ask when they saw the king in such distress. Jesus continues, "The King will reply, 'I tell you the truth, whatever you did for one of the least of these brothers of mine, you did for me' " (vv. 34-40, NIV). Then the Son of Man will reject the goats because they did not do these things for the king, and when the goats ask when they did not help the king when he was in distress, the king will reply that not doing it for the least of the brethren meant they did not do it for the king. Describing the fate of the goats, Jesus says, "Then they will go away to eternal punishment, but the righteous to eternal life" (vv. 41-46, NIV).

Calvin reflects on these verses in his *Commentary*. He suggests that Christ is providing an example of the types of duties of charity "by which we give evidence that we fear God." Calvin suggests that if a person were to do these types of activities apart from justification by faith, such actions would not be of any help for the individual's salvation, since the person's basic separation from God has not yet been dealt with. However, for the Christian, such actions are to be expected because, "unquestionably believers not only profess with the mouth, but prove by actual performances, that they serve God."[70]

Calvin goes on to assert that Jesus "does not exclude those duties which belong to the worship of God" but that he does tell his disciples "that it will be an authentic evidence of a holy life, if they practise charity..."[71]

Luke 6:46 and Matthew 7:21. Calvin has a similar comment about Jesus' question, in Luke 6:46, "Why do you call me 'Lord, Lord,' and do not do what I say?" (NIV). In Matthew 7:21, Jesus makes a statement rather than asks a question: "Not everyone who says to me, 'Lord, Lord,' will enter the kingdom of heaven, but only the one who does the will of my Father in heaven..." (NRSV). Calvin writes, "*To do the will of the Father* not only means, to regulate their life and manners, (as philosophers talked,) by the rule of virtues, but also to believe in Christ... These words, therefore, do not exclude faith, but presuppose it as the principle from which other good works flow" [italics in original].[72]

Acts 26: 19-20. In Acts 26:19-23, the Apostle Paul is defending himself before King Agrippa. In just a few verses he summarizes his entire ministry. Verses 19 and 20 read,

> "So then, King Agrippa, I was not disobedient to the vision from heaven. First to those in Damascus, then to those in Jerusalem and in all Judea, and to the Gentiles also, I preached that they should repent and turn to God and prove their repentance by their deeds" (NIV).

Calvin comments, "Conversion, or turning unto God, is joined with repentance... And because repentance is an inward thing, and placed in the affection of the heart, Paul requireth, in the second place, such works as may make the same known, according to that exhortation of John the Baptist: 'Bring forth fruits meet for repentance' (Matth. iii. 8)."[73]

---

[70] John Calvin, *Commentary of the Harmony of the Evangelists, Matthew, Mark, and Luke*, William Pringle, trans. (Edinburgh, Scotland: The Calvin Translation Society, 1846), 179.

[71] Calvin, *Commentary of the Harmony of the Evangelists*, 180.

[72] Calvin, *Commentary of the Harmony of the Evangelists*, 367-368.

[73] John Calvin, *Commentary Upon the Acts of the Apostles*, Henry Beveridge, ed. (Edinburgh, Scotland: T. & T. Clark, 1859), 322.

Calvin's comment regarding this verse in Acts continues the theme stated regarding the verses from Matthew 25 and Luke 6. That is, the experience of grace will be evident in behavior consistent with the internal condition.

Ephesians 2:8-10. The same idea is developed by both Calvin and Luther as they comment on a passage that is often cited as a key statement of justification by grace alone. Ephesians 2: 8-9 reads,

> For it is by grace you have been saved, through faith—and this not from yourselves, it is the gift of God—not by works so that no one can boast (NIV).

Luther comments on the passage, "God looks at this sin of the nature alone. This can be eradicated by no law, by no punishment; the grace of God alone, which makes the nature pure and new, must purge it away. The law only makes it manifest and teaches how to recognize it, but does not save from it... Therefore he first gives the law, by which man recognizes this sin and thirsts for grace; then he also gives the gospel and saves him."[74]

The verse immediately following Ephesians 2:8 and 9, verse 10, reads, "For we are God's workmanship, created in Christ Jesus to do good works, which God prepared in advance for us to do" (NIV). In his lectures on Genesis, Luther reflected on this verse in the context of the "comedy" of Joseph and his brothers (Gen. 44:17). Luther wrote, "For such is the nature of God's poems, as Paul neatly says in Eph. 2:10: 'We are His ποίημα.' God is the Poet, and we are the verses or songs He writes. Accordingly, there is no doubt that all our works and actions are pleasing in God's eyes on account of the special power and grace of faith."[75]

In his *Commentary*, Calvin reflects on Ephesians 2:10 as follows: "for all the good works which we possess are the fruit of regeneration. Hence it follows, that works themselves are a part of grace." He continues, "Everything in us, therefore, that is good, is the supernatural gift of God... *We are his work*, because we have been *created*,—not in Adam, but *in Christ Jesus*,—not to every kind of life, but to *good works*" [italics in original]. Calvin goes on to state that the works were "prepared" in the sense that God "draws" these works "out of his treasures, in which they had long before been laid up; for whom he called, them he justifies and regenerates."[76]

Dietrich Bonhoeffer, from his mid-twentieth century perspective in a nation that was gearing up for war, was able to affirm the same conclusions from these verses. He wrote, "That indeed is the whole purpose of our new creation in Christ... All this is perfectly clear: the aim of the Christian life is to produce those good works which God demands... But ultimately there is only one good work; the work of God in Christ Jesus... But all our good works are the works of God himself, the works for which he has prepared us beforehand."[77]

---

[74] John Sander, ed., *Devotional Readings from Luther's Works for Every Day of the Year* (Rock Island, IL: Augustana Book Concern, 1915), 9.

[75] Jaroslav Pelikan, ed., *Luther's Works, Vol. 7: Lectures on Genesis Chapters 38-44* (St. Louis, MO: Concordia Publishing House, 1965), 366.

[76] John Calvin, *Commentaries on the Epistles of Paul to the Galatians and Ephesians*, William Pringle, trans. (Edinburgh, Scotland: The Calvin Translation Society, 1854), 229, 231.

[77] Bonhoeffer, 333-334.

James 2. Late in his life, Luther voiced serious reservations about the book of James.[78] Nevertheless, he reflected on passages from the book in his devotional writings. Calvin, on the other hand, indicates that he can "see no just cause for rejecting it."[79] Yet both men commented on the second chapter in which the issue of faith and works is discussed in some detail. Following are comments on a few of the verses that have bearing on the present discussion.

James 2:15-16 reads, "Suppose a brother or sister is without clothes and daily food. If one of you says to him, 'Go, I wish you well; keep warm and well fed,' but does nothing about his physical needs, what good is it?" (NIV). Calvin reflects, "As, then, he who sends away a poor man with words, and offers him no help, treats him with mockery, so they who devise for themselves faith without works, and without any of the duties of religion, trifle with God."[80]

Regarding James 2:17—"In the same way, faith by itself, if it is not accompanied by action, is dead" (NIV)—Luther wrote that Christ is seen in good works among "the blind, the deaf, the lame, the lepers, the dead and the poor." Our own works are not worthy of God, but the works of Christ are acceptable. "God demands of us no other work that we should do for him than to exercise faith in Christ." Being confident that this action of believing in Christ is all that is required before God, Luther then admonishes the reader,

> Look for the poor, sick and all kinds of needy, help them and let your life's energy appear in this, so that they may enjoy your kindness, helping wherever your help is needed, as much as you possibly can with your life, property and honor. Know that to serve God is nothing else than to serve your neighbor in love, whether he be enemy or friend, or whether you can help in temporal or spiritual matters. This is serving God and doing good works.[81]

Calvin's comments are more concise: "We hence conclude that it is indeed no faith, for when dead, it does not properly retain the name."[82]

Calvin is equally direct when he comments on the James 2:18 statement, "But someone will say, 'You have faith; I have deeds.' Show me your faith without deeds, and I will show you my faith by what I do" (NIV). Calvin states "the design of James was to expose the foolish boasting of those who imagined that they had faith when by their life they shewed that they were unbelievers." He goes on to say, "This only he means, that faith, without the evidence of good works, is vainly pretended, because fruit ever comes from the living root of a good tree."[83]

Calvin also reflects on James holding up Abraham in chapter 2, verse 22, "his faith was made complete by what he did" (NIV). Calvin explains this comment by saying, "It is

---

[78] Martin Luther, *Table Talk*, Theodore G. Tappert, ed. (Philadelphia: Fortress Press, 1967), Vol. 54, 424-425.

[79] John Calvin, "Commentaries on the Catholic Epistles," John Owen, ed., in *Calvin's Commentaries Vol. 22, Hebrews, 1 Peter, 1 John, James, 2 Peter, Jude* (Grand Rapids, MI: Baker Book House, 1984), 276.

[80] Calvin, "Catholic Epistles," 310-311.

[81] Sander, 439-440.

[82] Calvin, "Catholic Epistles," 311.

[83] Calvin, "Catholic Epistles," 311, 312.

said to have been perfected by works, not because it received thence its own perfection, but because it was thus proved to be true."[84]

Luther considers James 2:26 which reads, "As the body without the spirit is dead, so faith without deeds is dead" (NIV). Luther wrote, "Faith is an active, living thing. But in order that men may not deceive themselves and think they have faith when they have not, they are to examine their works, whether they also love their neighbors and do good to them."[85]

Calvin does not explicitly comment on this last verse in chapter two, but closes his reflection on that chapter by saying, "We, indeed, allow, that good works are required for righteousness; we only take away from them the power of conferring righteousness, because they cannot stand before the tribunal of God."[86]

Table 29, at the end of this chapter, provides a partial list of verses which are relevant to this topic of the relationship between faith and works.

Diagnosing the Condition A review of these few verses raises another issue. That is, it is apparently possible to confess to having faith, and yet not have it.

Calvin alluded to this situation in the *Institutes* when he wrote, "At that time [in the early church] there were many—and this tends to be a perpetual evil in the church—who openly disclosed their unbelief by neglecting and overlooking all the proper works of believers, yet did not cease to boast of the false name of faith."[87]

Elsewhere, he wrote about the role of works in helping to identify those whose faith was sincere. "As piety lies within the heart, and as God does not dwell amongst us in order to make trial of our *love* towards Him, and does not even need our services, it is easy for hypocrites to lie, and falsely to pretend to *love God*. But the duties of brotherly love fall under the senses, and are placed before the eyes of all, and therefore in them the impudence of hypocrites is better ascertained" [italics in the original].[88]

In a similar way, Luther argues in "The Disputation Concerning Justification," that works are a valid sign of grace: "Works only reveal faith, just as fruits only show the tree, whether it is a good tree. For the works indicate whether I have faith. I conclude, therefore, that he is righteous, when I see that he does good works. In God's eyes that distinction is not necessary, for he is not deceived by hypocrisy. But it is necessary among men, so that they may correctly understand where faith is and where it is not."[89]

In a reflection on Matthew 23:24, Calvin is disturbed about some in the church who would "strain out a gnat but swallow a camel" (NRSV). His disdain for those who debate rather than pursue the higher calling of the faith is expressed as follows:

> But it is evident that hypocrites amuse themselves with such distinctions; for
> while they pass by *judgment, mercy and faith,* and even tear in pieces the whole

---

[84] Calvin, "Catholic Epistles," 315.

[85] Sander, 352.

[86] Calvin, "Catholic Epistles," 317.

[87] Calvin, *Institutes*, 815.

[88] Calvin, *Harmony of the Evangelists*, 91.

[89] Lewis W. Spitz, ed., *Luther's Works, Volume 34, Career of the Reformer IV* (Philadelphia: Fortress Press, 1960), 161.

Law, they are excessively rigid and severe in matters that are of no great importance; and while in this way they pretend to kiss the feet of God, they proudly spit in his face [italics in original].[90]

Calvin would therefore seem to indicate that there are those who number themselves among the church but who, in fact, do not possess the faith that will justify them before God.

Writing four centuries later, Bonhoeffer voiced a similar opinion when he wrote, "But not everyone who makes this confession will enter the kingdom of heaven. The dividing line will run right through the confessing Church. Even if we make the confession of faith, it gives us no title to any special claim on Jesus. We can never appeal to our confession or be saved simply on the ground that we have made it." Bonhoeffer then contrasts the person who says "Lord, Lord" and the person who humbly obeys. Bonhoeffer says the first "justifies himself through his confession… [he] has called himself to Jesus without the Holy Spirit, or else he has made out of the call of Jesus a personal privilege." The second's "doing is a token of grace to which there can be no other response save that of humble and obedient service."[91]

There is no question that faith saves, and confessing that faith is a necessary step in the process. However, it would appear that not all who say the words actually have faith.

The relationship between a consistent lifestyle and the confession of faith has also been a prominent issue in recent history. The "confessing church" that Dietrich Bonhoeffer referred to grew out of what was called the "German church struggle." A recent article stated, "The struggle was perceived and articulated by the Synod of Barmen in terms of confessionalism versus accommodation to culture…" in this case, to the growing commitment to Nazism in pre-World War II Germany.[92]

Leaders still struggle with the role of the church and church members during the Holocaust. Recently, Bartholomeos I, ecumenical patriarch of the Orthodox Church, visited the Holocaust Museum in Washington, DC. At that time, he was reported to have said, "The bitter truth for so many Christians of that terrible time was they could not connect the message of their faith to their actions in the world."[93]

Another recent example where significant aspects of the church yielded to accommodation to culture in the face of great evil was the struggle with apartheid in South Africa. The Dutch Reformed Church, which supported South Africa's previous racist regime, was suspended from the World Alliance of Reformed Churches in 1982. An article in *The National Christian Reporter*, stated if the Dutch Reformed Church's "governing body rejects apartheid 'in its fundamental nature,'…the church is expected to be voted back into membership in the World Alliance of Reformed Churches."[94]

Also related to the apartheid struggle, a Catholic News Service article indicated that the Catholic Church in South Africa has also confessed, at the Truth and Reconciliation

---

[90] Calvin, *Harmony of the Evangelists*, 93.

[91] Bonhoeffer, 215.

[92] James R. Edwards, "At the Crossroads," *Christianity Today*, August 11, 1997, pp. 22-23.

[93]"Between East and West," *The Christian Century*, November 5, 1997, 999.

[94] Stephen Brown, "Reformed Group Says 'Struggle for Economic Justice at Center of Faith,' " *The National Christian Reporter*, August 29, 1997, 1.

Commission hearings, its own lack of appropriate action while apartheid was in effect. " 'The complicity of the church…is found in acts of omission rather than commission…Silence in the face of ongoing and systematic oppression at all levels of society is perhaps the church's greatest sin,' said the document, drawn up by Father Sean O'Leary, head of the Southern African Catholic Bishops' Conference's justice and peace commission."[95]

Reviewing these historical tragedies raises the question, in the context of the present discussion, as to whether the church in the U.S. is confronted with a contemporary sin of omission. Consider the following facts:

- As indicated in chapter one of this report, between 1968 and 1995, while income increased by 68% after taxes and inflation, church member giving increased by 33%. As a result, the portion of income donated to the church declined by 21%.

- Of the additional money donated to the church between 1968 and 1995, 97% of the inflation-adjusted increase went into Congregational Finances, primarily to benefit current members of the church.

- Global communications systems provide information about world conditions. As a result, it is no secret that 35,000 children under the age of five die daily around the globe, mostly from preventable poverty conditions, and many in areas where there is not even a "cell" of the church, to use a World Council of Churches phrase, or where people are "unreached" with the Gospel, to use an evangelical term.

- While the portion of income going to the church declined, credit card interest payments increased 463% per capita between 1975 and 1991, the last years for which data is readily available.

- In the early 1990s, while the average church member spent less than $20 a year on global outreach—including activities that provide temporal and spiritual aid to the children dying around the globe—Americans, including church members, spent an average of $164 on soft drinks, $657 on restaurant meals, and over $1,000 on recreation activities per person.

- In most congregations, 20% of the people give 50-80% of the budget; there are indications that, in a number of congregations, one-third to one-half give no financial assistance to support their church.

Does the above data describe a challenge to the church in the U.S. on a par with the German church struggle and apartheid? How should the comments of Luther, Calvin and Bonhoeffer about the place of works as a fruit of faith be interpreted in light of these facts?

The same August 29, 1997 issue of *The National Christian Reporter* that had an article about the Reformed Church in South Africa also reported from Debrecen, Hungary that the World Alliance of Reformed Churches called its member churches "to recognize that the struggle against economic injustice and ecological destruction is at the very center of Christian faith…" The article went on,

---

[95] Catholic News Service, Cape Town, South Africa reported in *The Catholic Post*, September 7, 1997, 2.

These same issues were being "elevated" from moral and ethical questions to the "level of the faith" and the "confession" of the church...a situation described as a processus confessionis (a Latin term referring to a "committed process of progressive recognition, education and confession").

The general council has made a clear parallel between the rejection of economic injustice and the rejection of apartheid.[96]

The church in the U.S. may need to reconsider its current giving patterns in terms of this elevation of economic discipleship to a higher level of theological review. However, the question may be asked, is it fair to judge church members at all? Further, if one were to make a determination about the sincerity of faith of church members, would economic justice issues, or more particularly in the present discussion, church member giving patterns be a valid measure?

Regarding the appropriateness of judging the church, comments from Bonhoeffer once again may be relevant. He wrote, "In other words the preaching of forgiveness must always go hand-in-hand with the preaching of repentance... It is the will of the Lord himself that the gospel should not be given to the dogs." Bonhoeffer went on to advise that "brotherly admonition" within the church is critical for the health of the church. "This is the only form of protection against our daily trials and temptations, and against apostasy within the congregation."[97]

In terms of church giving as a basis for considering the sincerity of church member faith, Jesus seems to recommend that idea in Matthew 6:21. In this section of the Sermon on the Mount, Jesus is talking about the believer's relationship to God and Mammon, which word is translated as "money" in modern versions of the Bible. Telling those listening to store up treasures in heaven rather than on earth, Jesus says, "For where your treasure is, there your heart will be also" (NRSV). This verse seems to indicate that the way a believer spends money may be the clearest indication—perhaps like a thermometer—of the heart's spiritual condition.

If that is the case, then one might conclude that if one does not give money to the church to help others, one falls into the category of those who do not have the fruits that ought to accompany the presence of grace in their lives. And if the tree is not bearing fruit, is the root itself good?

This issue deserves serious consideration. If people are in the church with a false understanding of what it means to be a "believer," the consequences could be eternal. The December 3, 1997 issue of *The Christian Century* had two articles on hell. One, a biblical reflection on Luke 3:7-18, talks of hell as "going it alone, apart from God, all the way to the bitter end."[98] A second article notes that a majority of people believe in hell or think there might be one.[99]

Hell, of course, is an old-fashioned notion, so it is interesting that two articles mentioning it appeared in the same issue of a contemporary magazine. The biblical study,

[96] Brown, 1.
[97] Bonhoeffer, 324, 326.
[98] James F. Kay, "Unquenchable Fire," *The Christian Century*, December 3, 1997, 1121
[99] Martin E. Marty, "Certain Punishment," *The Christian Century*, December 3, 1997, 1143.

with the description of hell as separation from God, is fairly consistent with a description from the sixteenth century. Calvin provided more detail in his view, and yet emphasized the separation from Christ as a key element of hell: "We are therefore taught how desirable it is to be united to the Son of God; because everlasting destruction and the torment of the flesh await all those whom he will drive from his presence at the last day. He will then order the wicked to *depart* from him, because many hypocrites are now mixed with the righteous, as if they were closely allied to Christ" [italics in original].[100]

Even though a majority of Americans might agree with Calvin's general point, most would also see themselves as an exception to his view. A Gallup survey found that 73% of the U.S. population still believes there is a hell, but over three-quarters believe they won't go there.[101]

Yet, based on Jesus' statement in Matthew 6:21, and the earlier review of writings about works—that do not justify in and of themselves, but do necessarily flow out of grace, both as a response to it, and as a proof of it—then are many church members misinformed about their own spiritual prospects? From a strictly numerical point of view, as many as half the church members who do not invest in their churches financially do not have the fruit that accompanies the presence of grace in their lives.

If the giving numbers are a thermometer of heart condition, one would have to conclude that the fervor of church members is cooling, even as the portion of income given to the church declines. In previous chapters of this report, the potential of the church was discussed in contrast to current patterns. In that context, the tithe, or giving 10% of one's income to the church, was discussed. Of course, where grace abounds the tithe is only a guideline. In an affluent culture such as the United States, some even consider it a minimum. This ideal is in stark contrast to the patterns of the past 28 years.

Further, for the sake of discussion, consider what the numbers say about the possible condition of the church in the U.S. The data in the chapter on church giving by denominational affiliation might be useful in this context. For example, the denominations affiliated with the National Association of Evangelicals gave an average of 4% of their incomes to their churches in 1995. What is the best-case scenario for these churches? If one assumes that those who are contributing to the church are giving at the level of the classic tithe, or 10% of their incomes, the maximum number of members giving at least at the 10% level would be 40%. This formulation would mean that 60% of these denominations' members were giving less than 10% in an age of affluence, and therefore do not have the works of grace, indicating that they may be at risk of hell. Since it is unlikely that 40% of their members are tithing, it is probable that the giving is spread among more of the church membership at lower levels of giving. If this is true, then the number at risk grows, as more church members are not moving beyond the tithe to seek justice, grace and mercy, as Jesus describes in Matthew 23:23.

The level of giving for the National Council of Churches-affiliated denominations in the previous analysis was 3% in 1995. Therefore, the best-case scenario for these denominations

---

[100]Calvin, *Harmony of the Evangelists*, 182.

[101]"Many Believe in Hell (Far Fewer Expect to Go There)," *Princeton Religion Research Center Emerging Trends*, February 1995, 3.

would be that 30% of their members were giving at the 10% level. That would mean 70% of these denominations' members were giving less than 10% in an age of affluence, thus not evidencing the fruits of grace, and thus being at risk of negative eternal consequences. Once again, it is likely that the giving is not concentrated in 30% giving 10%, but rather is spread out at different levels throughout the congregations, meaning even a larger percent of the members are struggling with the integration of their faith with their actions, and being at risk of negative eternal consequences.

If church members who do not give to their churches do not have the fruits that accompany grace, they may not, in fact, have faith. They may be in that group who have the words but not the experience. If that is the case, what responsibility do church leaders have to provide these members with more accurate information about their spiritual state before it is too late?

The church in the United States has incredible potential for sharing abundant resources with a hurting world as a direct consequence of grace experienced through Jesus Christ. Yet giving patterns indicate that church members are investing a smaller portion of their lives in their churches as represented in the portion of their treasure that they contribute. Of the money that is invested, more is being spent internally in the congregation and less on the larger servanthood mission of the church. Further, other charitable giving data does not support the notion that people are giving less to the church in order to fund human service activities in non-church organizations.

Do these conditions describe a grace-filled church?

Or should church members be asking a question that was posed by one laywoman when the topic of giving to the church was under discussion. "If I am not trusting God with my money," she asked, "am I really trusting him with my eternal salvation?"

Table 29:   **A Partial List of Verse Citations Relevant to a Dialogue on Faith and Works**

Verses that Refer to Grace

John 1:17-18	Romans 8:1-3	2 Cor. 5:18-21	Col. 2:13-23	Heb. 10:1-23
John 3:16	Romans 8:10-11	Gal. 2:11-21	1 Th. 1:4	Heb. 12:24
John 3:36	Romans 8:26-39	Gal. 3	1 Th. 5:4-11	Heb. 13:12
John 5:24	Romans 9:11-33	Gal. 4:3-12	1 Th. 5:23-24	1 Peter 3:18
John 5:31-45	Romans 10:1-16	Gal. 4:21-31	2 Th. 2:13-14	1 John 1:8-10
Acts 15:9-11	Romans 11:5-6	Gal. 5:1-12	1 Tim. 2:5-6	1 John 2:1-2
Acts 18:27	Romans 14:10-13	Gal. 6:14-16	Titus 2:14a	1 John 2:12
Romans 1:17	Romans 15:8-9	Eph. 1	Titus 3:4-7	1 John 4:4-6
Romans 3:22	1 Cor. 1:2	Eph. 2	Heb. 2:9-10	1 John 4:10
Romans 3:24-28	1 Cor. 1:8-9	Eph. 3:12	Heb. 2:17-18	1 John 4:15
Romans 3:30	1 Cor. 1:30-31	Eph. 5:2	Heb. 4:14-16	1 John 5:11-12
Romans 3:31	1 Cor. 2:12	Phil. 3:2-11	Heb. 7:25	1 John 5:18
Romans 4	1 Cor. 3:5-15	Col. 1:6b	Heb. 8:6	Jude 1:24-25
Romans 5	1 Cor. 4:7	Col. 1:14	Heb. 8:12	
Romans 7:21-25	1 Cor. 5:5	Col. 1:19-22	Heb. 9	

Verses that Refer to Obedience

Mat. 3:7-11	Luke 17:5, 10	1 Cor. 6:9-20	1 Tim. 4:1-2	1 Peter 2:15
Mat. 6:21-24	Luke 19:8-10	1 Cor. 9:24-27	1 Tim. 5:15	1 Peter 2:16
Mat. 7:21	John 3:36	1 Cor. 15:32-34	1 Tim. 5:24	1 Peter 2:24
Mat. 7:15-27	John 5:29	2 Cor. 5:7-11	1 Tim. 6:9-10	1 Peter 4:10
Mat. 13:22	John 6:28-29	2 Cor. 5:17	2 Tim. 2:15-18	1 Peter 4:18
Mat. 13:24-29	John 8:31	2 Cor. 8:8	2 Tim. 3:1-13	2 Peter 1:3-4
Mat. 13:36-43	John 13:17	2 Cor. 9:13	2 Tim. 4:1-4	2 Peter 1:5-11
Mat. 16:24-27	John 13:34-35	2 Cor. 11:13-15	Titus 1:10-16	2 Peter 2:19-22
Mat. 19:16-28	John 14:10-14	2 Cor. 11:26c	Titus 2:14b	1 John 1:5-7
Mat. 21:28-31	John 14:17	2 Cor. 13:5-6	Titus 3:8	1 John 2:3-6
Mat. 22:34-40	John 14:21	Gal. 2:4	Philemon 1:6	1 John 2:9-11
Mat. 23:23	John 14:23-24	Gal. 2:10	Heb. 2:1-3	1 John 2:15-17
Mat. 24:36-51	John 15:9-17	Gal. 5:6b	Heb. 3:5-19	I John 3:1-24
Mat. 25:31-46	John 17:17	Gal. 5:13-26	Heb. 4:1-13	1 John 4:8
Mark 4:13-20	Acts 14:3	Gal. 6:7-10	Heb. 5:8-9	1 John 4:11
Mark 8:34-38	Acts 26:20b	Gal. 6:15b	Heb. 6:1-12	1 John 4:16-18
Mark 13:33-37	Rom. 6	Eph. 2:10	Heb. 10:24-39	1 John 4:19-21
Luke 6:43-45	Rom. 7:4-6	Eph. 4:21-32	Heb. 11:1	1 John 5:1-5
Luke 6:46-49	Rom. 8:4-9	Eph. 5:5-9	Heb. 11:7-8	2 John 5-7
Luke 8:11-15	Rom. 8:12-14	Phil. 1:11	Heb. 12:14-15	3 John 1:11
Luke 8:19-21	Rom. 10:21	Phil. 2:12-13	Heb. 12:25	Jude 1:4-19
Luke 11:27-28	Rom. 11:22	Phil. 3:17-21	James 1:22-27	Rev. 3
Luke 12:16-21	Rom. 12:1-2	Col. 1:23	James 2:14-26	Rev. 14:9-12
Luke 12:22-34	Rom. 13:11-14	Col. 2:6-7	James 4:1-4	Rev. 19:7-8
Luke 12:35-48	Rom. 15:7	Col. 3:5-10	James 5:1-6	Rev. 20:11-15
Luke 13:22-27	1 Cor. 3:1-5	Col. 3:25	1 Peter 1:2	Rev. 22:12-13
Luke 14:25-35	1 Cor. 4:2-5	1 Thes. 1:5-10	1 Peter 1:14-17	
Luke 16:8-13	1 Cor. 4:19-20	1 Thes. 4:6-8	1 Peter 1:17-22	
Luke 16:19-31	1 Cor. 5:9-13	1 Tim. 1:19-20	1 Peter 2:8-12	

Two versions of Scripture were used in the verses quoted in the body of the text:

The Holy Bible: New International Version © 1978 by the New York International Bible Society, used by permission of Zondervan Bible Publishers.
New Revised Standard Version Bible, © 1989, by the Division of Christian Education of the National Council of the Churches of Christ in the United States of America.

Appendixes

Appendix A: List of Denominations

Church Member Giving, 1968-1995

American Baptist Churches in the U.S.A.
Associate Reformed Presbyterian Church
  (General Synod)
Brethren in Christ Church
Christian Church (Disciples of Christ)
Church of God (Anderson, Ind.)
Church of God General Conference (Oregon, IL and
  Morrow, GA.)
Church of the Brethren
Church of the Nazarene
Conservative Congregational Christian Conference
Cumberland Presbyterian Church
Evangelical Congregational Church
Evangelical Covenant Church
Evangelical Lutheran Church in America
  The American Lutheran Church (merged 1987)
  Lutheran Church in America (merged 1987)
Evangelical Lutheran Synod
Evangelical Mennonite Church
Fellowship of Evangelical Bible Churches
Free Methodist Church of North America
Friends United Meeting (through 1990)
General Association of General Baptists
Lutheran Church-Missouri Synod
Mennonite Church
Moravian Church in America, Northern Province
North American Baptist Conference
The Orthodox Presbyterian Church
Presbyterian Church (U.S.A.)
Reformed Church in America
Seventh-day Adventists
Southern Baptist Convention
United Church of Christ
Wisconsin Evangelical Lutheran Synod

Church Member Giving, 1994–1995

The Denominations included in the 1968-1995
  analysis plus the following:
Albanian Orthodox Diocese of America
Allegheny Wesleyan Methodist Connection
  (Original Allegheny Conference)
Apostolic Faith Mission Church of God
Baptist Missionary Association of America
Christian and Missionary Alliance
Church of Lutheran Brethren of America

Church of the Lutheran Confession
Churches of God General Conference
The Episcopal Church
The Evangelical Church
General Conference Mennonite Brethren Church
International Pentecostal Church of Christ
International Pentecostal Holiness Church
The Latvian Evangelical Lutheran Church in America
The Missionary Church
Primitive Methodist Church in the U.S.A.
The Schwenkfelder Church
United Brethren in Christ
The United Methodist Church
The Wesleyan Church

By Organizational Affiliation: NAE, 1968-1995

Brethren in Christ Church
Church of the Nazarene
Conservative Congregational Christian Conference
Evangelical Congregational Church
Evangelical Mennonite Church
Fellowship of Evangelical Bible Churches
Free Methodist Church of North America
General Association of General Baptists

By Organizational Affiliation: NCC, 1968-1995

American Baptist Churches in the U.S.A.
Christian Church (Disciples of Christ)
Church of the Brethren
Evangelical Lutheran Church in America
Moravian Church in America, Northern Province
Presbyterian Church (U.S.A.)
Reformed Church in America
United Church of Christ

Eleven Denominations, 1921-1995

American Baptist (Northern)
Christian Church (Disciples of Christ)
Church of the Brethren
The Episcopal Church
Evangelical Lutheran Church in America
  The American Lutheran Church
    American Lutheran Church
    The Evangelical Lutheran Church

United Evangelical Lutheran Church
Lutheran Free Church
Evangelical Lutheran Churches, Assn. of
Lutheran Church in America
   United Lutheran Church
      General Council Evangelical Lutheran Ch.
      General Synod of Evangelical Lutheran Ch.
      United Synod Evangelical Lutheran South
   American Evangelical Lutheran Church
   Augustana Lutheran Church
   Finnish Lutheran Church (Suomi Synod)
Moravian Church in America, Northern Province
Presbyterian Church (U.S.A.)
   United Presbyterian Church in the U.S.A.
     Presbyterian Church in the U.S.A.
     United Presbyterian Church in North America
   Presbyterian Church in the U.S.
Reformed Church in America
Southern Baptist Convention
United Church of Christ
   Congregational Christian
   Congregational
   Evangelical and Reformed
     Evangelical Synod of North America/German
     Reformed Church in the U.S.
The United Methodist Church
   The Evangelical United Brethren
   The Methodist Church
     Methodist Episcopal Church
     Methodist Episcopal Church South
     Methodist Protestant Church

Christian and Missionary Alliance
Church of God (Anderson, IN)
Church of God (Cleveland, Tenn.)
Church of God, Gen. Conf. (Oregon, IL and Morrow, GA)
Church of the Nazarene
Conservative Cong. Christian Conf.
Cumberland Presbyterian Church
Evangelical Congregational Church
Evangelical Covenant Church
Evangelical Lutheran Synod
Evangelical Mennonite Church
Fellowship of Evan. Bible Churches
Free Methodist Church of North America
General Association of General Baptists
Lutheran Church-Missouri Synod
Mennonite Church
North American Baptist Conference
The Orthodox Presbyterian Church
Salvation Army
Seventh-day Adventists
Southern Baptist Convention
Wisconsin Evangelical Lutheran Synod

Trends in Membership, 10 Mainline Protestant Denominations, 1968-1995

American Baptist Churches in the U.S.A.
Christian Church (Disciples of Christ)
Church of the Brethren
The Episcopal Church
Evangelical Lutheran Church in Am.
Moravian Church in America, Northern Prov.
Presbyterian Church (U.S.A.)
Reformed Church in America
United Church of Christ
The United Methodist Church

Trends in Membership, Add 26 Denominations, 1968-1995

Assemblies of God
Associate Reformed Presby. Ch (Gen Synod)
Baptist General Conference
Brethren in Christ Church

Appendix B Series: Denominational Data Tables

Introduction

The data in the following tables is from the *Yearbook of American and Canadian Churches* (*YACC*) series unless otherwise noted. Financial data is presented in current dollars.

The Appendix B tables are described below.

Appendix B-1, Church Member Giving, 1968-1995: This table presents data for the denominations which comprise the data set analyzed for the 1968 through 1995 period.

Elements of this data are also used for the analyses in chapters two through six.

In Appendix B-1, the data for the Presbyterian Church (U.S.A.) combined data for the United Presbyterian Church in the U.S.A. and the Presbyterian Church in the United States for the period 1968 through 1982. These two communions merged to become the Presbyterian Church (U.S.A.) in 1983, data for which is presented for 1983 through 1995.

Also in Appendix B-1, data for the Evangelical Lutheran Church in America appears beginning in 1987. Before that, the two major component communions that merged into that new denomination—the American Lutheran Church and the Lutheran Church in America—are listed as individual denominations from 1968 through 1986.

In the Appendix B series, the denomination listed as the Fellowship of Evangelical Bible Churches had been named the Evangelical Mennonite Brethren Church prior to July 1987.

The data for two denominations were obtained as follows.

Data for the American Baptist Churches in the U.S.A. has been obtained directly from the denominational office as follows. In discussions with the American Baptist Churches Office of Planning Resources, it became apparent that there had been no distinction made between the membership of congregations reporting financial data, and total membership for the denomination, when reporting data to the *Yearbook of American and Canadian Churches.* Records were obtained from the denomination for a smaller membership figure that reflected only those congregations reporting financial data. While this revised membership data provided a more useful per member giving figure for Congregational Finances, the total Benevolences figure reported to the *YACC,* while included in the present data set, does reflect contributions to some Benevolences categories from 100% of the American Baptist membership. The membership reported in Appendix B-1 for the American Baptist Churches is the membership for congregations reporting financial data, rather than the total membership figure provided in editions of the *Yearbook of American and Canadian Churches.* However, in the sections that consider membership as a percentage of population, the Total Membership figure for the American Baptist Churches is used.

Appendix B-2, Church Member Giving, 1994-1995: Appendix B-2 presents the Full or Confirmed Membership, Congregational Finances and Benevolences data for the twenty additional denominations included in the 1994-1995 comparison.

Appendix B-3, Church Member Giving for Eleven Denominations, 1921-1995: This appendix presents additional data which is not included in Appendix B-1 for the Eleven Denominations.

The data from 1921 through 1928 in Appendix B-3.1 is taken from summary information contained in the *Yearbook of American Churches, 1949 Edition*, George F. Ketcham, ed. (Lebanon, PA: Sowers Printing Company,

1949, p. 162). The summary membership data provided is for Inclusive Membership. Therefore, giving as a percentage of income for the years 1921 through 1928 may have been somewhat higher had Full or Confirmed Membership been used. The list of denominations that are summarized for this period is presented in the *Yearbook of American Churches, 1953 Edition*, Benson Y. Landis, ed. (New York: National Council of the Churches of Christ in the U.S.A., 1953, p. 274).

The data from 1929 through 1952 is taken from summary information presented in the *Yearbook of American Churches, Edition for 1955*, Benson Y. Landis, ed. (New York: National Council of the Churches of Christ in the U.S.A., 1954, pp. 286-287). A description of the list of denominations included in the 1929 through 1952 data summary on page 275 of the *YACC Edition for 1955* indicated that the Moravian Church, Northern Province is not included in the 1929 through 1952 data.

The data in Appendix B-3.2 for 1953 through 1964 was obtained for the indicated denominations from the relevant edition of the *YACC* series. Giving as a percentage of income was derived for these years by dividing the published Total Contributions figure by the published Per Capita figure to produce a membership figure for each denomination. The Total Contributions figures for the denominations were added to produce an aggregated Total Contributions figure. The calculated membership figures were also added to produce an aggregated membership figure. The aggregated Total Contributions figure was then divided by the aggregated membership figure to yield a per member giving figure which was used in calculating giving as a percentage of income.

Data for the years 1965 through 1967 was not available in a form that could be readily analyzed for the present purposes, and therefore data for these three years was estimated by dividing the change in per capita Total Contributions from 1964 to 1968 by four, the number of years in this interval, and cumulatively adding the result to the base year of 1964 and the succeeding years of 1965 and 1966 to obtain estimates for the years 1965 through 1967.

In most cases, this procedure was also applied to individual denominations to avoid an artificially low total due to missing data. If data was not available for a specific year, the otherwise blank entry was filled in with a calculation based on surrounding years for that denomination. For example, this procedure was used for the American Baptist Churches for the years 1955 and 1956, the Christian Church (Disciples of Christ) for the years 1955 and 1959, and the Evangelical United Brethren, later to merge into The United Methodist Church, for the years 1957, 1958 and 1959. Data for the Methodist Church was changed for 1957 in a similar manner.

Available Total Contributions and Full or Confirmed Members data for The Episcopal Church and The United Methodist Church for 1969 through 1995 is presented in Appendix B-3.3. These two communions are included in the Eleven Denominations. The United Methodist Church was created in 1968 when The Methodist Church and The Evangelical United Brethren Church merged. While The Methodist Church filed summary data for the year 1968, The Evangelical United Brethren Church did not. Data for these denominations was calculated as noted in the appendix. However, since the 1968 data for The Methodist Church would not have been comparable to the 1985 and 1995 data for The United Methodist Church, this communion was not included in the more focused 1968-1995 analysis.

Appendix B-1: Church Member Giving 1968-1995

Key to Denominational Abbreviations: Data Years 1968-1995

Abbreviation	Denomination
abc	American Baptist Churches in the U.S.A.
alc	The American Lutheran Church
arp	Associate Reformed Presbyterian Church (General Synod)
bcc	Brethren in Christ Church
ccd	Christian Church (Disciples of Christ)
cga	Church of God (Anderson, IN)
cgg	Church of God General Conference (Oregon, IL)
chb	Church of the Brethren
chn	Church of the Nazarene
ccc	Conservative Congregational Christian Conference
cpc	Cumberland Presbyterian Church
ecc	Evangelical Congregational Church
ecv	Evangelical Covenant Church
elc	Evangelical Lutheran Church in America
els	Evangelical Lutheran Synod
emc	Evangelical Mennonite Church
feb	Fellowship of Evangelical Bible Churches
fmc	Free Methodist Church of North America
fum	Friends United Meeting
ggb	General Association of General Baptists
lca	Lutheran Church in America
lms	Lutheran Church-Missouri Synod
mch	Mennonite Church
mca	Moravian Church in America, Northern Province
nab	North American Baptist Conference
opc	The Orthodox Presbyterian Church
pch	Presbyterian Church (U.S.A.)
rca	Reformed Church in America
sda	Seventh-day Adventists
sbc	Southern Baptist Convention
ucc	United Church of Christ
wel	Wisconsin Evangelical Lutheran Synod

Appendix B-1: Church Member Giving, 1968-1995 (continued)

	Data Year 1968			Data Year 1969			Data Year 1970		
	Full/Confirmed Members	Congregational Finances	Benevolences	Full/Confirmed Members	Congregational Finances	Benevolences	Full/Confirmed Members	Congregational Finances	Benevolences
abc	1,179,848 [a]	95,878,267 [a]	21,674,924 [a]	1,153,785 [a]	104,084,322	21,111,333	1,231,944 [a]	112,668,310	19,655,391
alc	1,767,618	137,260,390	32,862,410	1,771,999	143,917,440	34,394,570	1,775,573	146,268,320	30,750,030
arp	28,312	2,239,825	1,274,348	28,273	2,943,214	978,097	NA	NA	NA
bcc	8,954	1,645,256	633,200 [a]	9,145	1,795,859	817,445	NA	NA	NA
ccd	994,683	105,803,222	21,703,947	936,931	91,169,842	18,946,815	911,964	98,671,692	17,386,032
cga	146,807	23,310,682	4,168,580	147,752	24,828,448	4,531,678	150,198	26,962,037	4,886,223
cgg	6,600	805,000	103,000	6,700	805,000	104,000	6,800	810,000	107,000
chb	187,957	12,975,829	4,889,727	185,198	13,964,158 [a]	4,921,991 [a]	182,614	14,327,896	4,891,618
chn	364,789	59,943,750 [a]	14,163,761 [a]	372,943	64,487,669 [a]	15,220,339 [a]	383,284	68,877,922 [a]	16,221,123 [a]
ccc	15,127	1,867,978	753,686	16,219	1,382,195	801,534	17,328	1,736,818	779,696
cpc	86,729 [a]	5,542,678 [a]	906,583 [a]	88,091	6,393,665	1,020,248	NA	NA	NA
ecc	29,239	2,464,760	610,056	29,582	2,660,674	627,732	NA	NA	NA
ecv	66,021	11,923,084	3,072,848	67,522	12,168,837	3,312,306	67,441	13,309,618	3,578,876
elc	ALC & LCA	ALC & LCA	ALC & LCA	ALC & LCA	ALC & LCA	ALC & LCA	ALC & LCA	ALC & LCA	ALC & LCA
els	10,886 [a]	844,235 [a]	241,949 [a]	11,079	1,003,746	315,325	11,030	969,625	295,349
emc	2,870 [a]	447,397	232,331	NA	NA	NA	NA	NA	NA
feb	1,712 [a]	156,789 [a]	129,818 [a]	3,324	389,000	328,000	3,698	381,877	706,398
fmc	47,831 [a]	12,032,016 [a]	2,269,677 [a]	47,954 [a]	9,152,729	7,495,653	64,901	9,641,202	7,985,264
fum	55,469	3,564,793	1,256,192	55,257	3,509,509	1,289,026	53,970	3,973,802	1,167,183
ggb	65,000	4,303,183 [a]	269,921 [a]	NA	NA	NA	NA	NA	NA
lca	2,279,383	166,337,149	39,981,858	2,193,321	161,958,669	46,902,225	2,187,015	169,795,380	42,118,870
lms	1,877,799	178,042,762	47,415,800	1,900,708	185,827,626	49,402,590	1,922,569	193,352,322	47,810,664
mch	85,682	7,304,585	5,179,023 [a]	85,343	7,398,182	6,038,730	NA	NA	NA
mca	27,772	2,583,354	444,910	27,617	2,642,529	456,182	27,173	2,704,105	463,219
nab	42,371 [a]	5,176,669 [a]	1,383,964 [a]	55,100	6,681,410	2,111,588	55,080	6,586,929	2,368,288
opc	9,197	1,638,437	418,102	9,276	1,761,242	464,660	NA	NA	NA
pch	4,180,093	375,248,474	102,622,450	4,118,664	388,268,169	97,897,522	4,041,813	401,785,731	93,927,852
rca	226,819 [a]	25,410,489 [a]	9,197,642 [a]	224,992 [a]	27,139,579 [a]	9,173,312	223,353 [a]	29,421,849 [a]	9,479,503 [a]
sda	395,159 [a]	36,976,280	95,178,335	407,766	40,378,426	102,730,594	420,419	45,280,059	109,569,241
sbc	11,332,229 [a]	666,924,020 [a]	128,023,731 [a]	11,487,708	709,246,590	133,203,885	11,628,032	753,510,973	138,480,329
ucc	2,032,648 [a]	152,301,536	18,869,136	1,997,898	152,791,512	27,338,543	1,960,608	155,248,767	26,934,289
wel	259,954 [a]	19,000,023 [a]	6,574,308 [a]	265,069	20,786,613	6,417,042	271,117	22,582,545	6,810,612
Total	27,815,558	2,119,952,912	566,506,217	27,705,216	2,189,536,854	598,352,965	27,597,924	2,278,867,779	586,373,050

[a] Data obtained from denominational source.

104

Appendix B-1: Church Member Giving, 1968-1995 (continued)

	Data Year 1971			Data Year 1972			Data Year 1973		
	Full/Confirmed Members	Congregational Finances	Benevolences	Full/Confirmed Members	Congregational Finances	Benevolences	Full/Confirmed Members	Congregational Finances	Benevolences
abc	1,223,735 a	114,673,805	18,878,769	1,176,092 a	118,446,573	18,993,440	1,190,455 a	139,357,611 a	20,537,388
alc	1,775,774	146,324,460	28,321,740	1,773,414	154,786,570	30,133,850	1,770,119	168,194,730	35,211,440
arp	NA	NA	NA	NA	NA	NA	NA	NA	NA
bcc	9,550	2,357,786	851,725	9,730	2,440,400	978,957	NA	NA	NA
ccd	884,929	94,091,862	17,770,799	881,467	105,763,511	18,323,685	868,895	112,526,538	19,800,843
cga	152,787	28,343,604	5,062,282	155,920	31,580,751	5,550,487	157,828	34,649,592	6,349,695
cgg	7,200	860,000	120,000	7,400	900,000	120,000	7,440	940,000	120,000
chb	181,183	14,535,274	5,184,768	179,641	14,622,319 b	5,337,277 b	179,333	16,474,758	6,868,927
chn	394,197	75,107,918 a	17,859,332 a	404,732	82,891,903 a	20,119,679 a	417,200	91,318,469 a	22,661,140 a
ccc	19,416	1,903,865	937,572	20,400	1,983,364	1,002,765	21,014	2,116,291	1,066,277
cpc	57,147	6,848,115	1,139,480	56,212	8,449,593	554,843	56,584	9,715,351	847,727
ecc	29,652	3,001,867	646,187	29,682	3,563,512	742,292	29,434	3,469,890	798,968
ecv	68,428	14,857,190	3,841,887	69,815	14,557,206	4,169,053	69,922	15,500,129	4,259,950
elc	ALC & LCA	ALC & LCA	ALC & LCA	ALC & LCA	ALC & LCA	ALC & LCA	ALC & LCA	ALC & LCA	ALC & LCA
els	11,427	1,028,629	314,843	11,532	1,138,953	275,941	12,525	1,296,326	361,882
emc	NA	NA	NA	NA	NA	NA	3,131	593,070	408,440
feb	NA	NA	NA	NA	NA	NA	NA	NA	NA
fmc	65,040	13,863,601	6,092,503	48,455	15,206,381	6,638,789	48,763 a	17,483,258	7,000,353
fum	54,522	3,888,064	1,208,062	54,927	4,515,463	1,297,088	57,690	5,037,848	1,327,439
ggb	NA	NA	NA	NA	NA	NA	NA	NA	NA
lca	2,175,378	179,570,467	43,599,913	2,165,591	188,387,949	45,587,481	2,169,341	200,278,486	34,627,978
lms	1,945,889	203,619,804	48,891,368	1,963,262	216,756,345	50,777,670	1,983,114	230,435,598	54,438,074
mch	88,522	8,171,316	7,035,750	89,505	9,913,176	7,168,664	90,967	9,072,858	6,159,740
mca	26,101	2,576,172	459,447	25,500	2,909,252	465,316	25,468	3,020,667	512,424
nab	54,997	7,114,457	2,293,692	54,441	7,519,558	2,253,158	41,516	6,030,352	1,712,092
opc	NA	NA	NA	NA	NA	NA	NA	NA	NA
pch	3,963,665	420,865,807	93,164,548	3,855,494	436,042,890	92,691,469	3,730,312 c	480,735,088 c	95,462,247 c
rca	219,915 a	32,217,319 a	9,449,655 a	217,583 a	34,569,814 a	9,508,818 a	212,906 a	39,524,443 a	10,388,619 a
sda	433,906	49,208,043	119,913,879	449,188	54,988,781	132,411,980	464,276	60,643,602	149,994,942
sbc	11,824,676	814,406,626	160,510,775	12,065,333	896,427,208	174,711,648	12,295,400	1,011,467,569	193,511,983
ucc	1,928,674	158,924,956	26,409,521	1,895,016	165,556,364	27,793,561	1,867,810	168,602,602	28,471,058
wel	275,500	24,365,692	7,481,644	278,442	26,649,585	8,232,320	283,130	29,450,094	8,650,699
Total	27,872,210	2,422,726,699	627,440,141	27,938,774	2,600,567,481	665,840,231	28,054,573	2,857,935,220	711,550,325

[a] Data obtained from denominational source.

[b] YACC Church of the Brethren figures reported for 15 months due to fiscal year change; adjusted here to 12/15ths.

[c] The Presbyterian Church (USA) data for 1973 combines United Presbyterian Church in the U.S.A. data for 1973 (see YACC 1975) and an average of Presbyterian Church in the United States data for 1972 and 1974, since 1973 data was not reported in the YACC series.

Appendix B-1: Church Member Giving, 1968-1995 (continued)

	Data Year 1974			Data Year 1975			Data Year 1976		
	Full/Confirmed Members	Congregational Finances	Benevolences	Full/Confirmed Members	Congregational Finances	Benevolences	Full/Confirmed Members	Congregational Finances	Benevolences
abc	1,176,989 a	147,022,280	21,847,285	1,180,793 a	153,697,091	23,638,372	1,142,773 a	163,134,092	25,792,357
alc	1,764,186	173,318,574	38,921,546	1,764,810	198,863,519	75,666,809	1,768,758	215,527,544	76,478,278
arp	28,570	3,753,120	1,050,697	28,589	4,090,321	961,760	28,581	4,370,831	1,118,783
bcc	10,255	3,002,218	1,078,576	10,784	3,495,152	955,845	11,375	4,088,492	1,038,484
ccd	854,844	119,434,435	20,818,434	859,885	126,553,931	22,126,459	845,058	135,008,269	23,812,274
cga	161,401	39,189,287	7,343,123	166,259	42,077,029	7,880,559	170,285	47,191,302	8,854,295
cgg	7,455	975,000	105,000	7,485	990,000	105,000	7,620	1,100,000	105,000
chb	179,387	18,609,614	7,281,551	179,336	20,338,351	7,842,819 b	178,157	22,133,858	8,032,293
chn	430,128	104,774,391	25,534,267 a	441,093	115,400,881	28,186,392 a	448,658	128,294,499	32,278,187 a
ccc	21,975	2,489,571	1,194,417	22,349	2,692,651	1,764,264	21,977	3,137,553	1,505,044
cpc	55,577	9,619,526	1,087,680	90,005	11,392,729	1,215,279	88,382	10,919,882	1,648,770
ecc	29,331	3,928,781	896,828	29,636	4,182,648	1,009,726	28,886	4,503,104	1,068,134
ecv	69,960	17,044,074	5,131,124	71,808	19,875,977	6,353,422	73,458	21,451,544	6,898,871
elc	ALC & LCA	ALC & LCA	ALC & LCA	ALC & LCA	ALC & LCA	ALC & LCA	ALC & LCA	ALC & LCA	ALC & LCA
els	13,097	1,519,749	394,725	13,480	1,739,255	573,000	14,504	2,114,998	456,018
emc	3,123	644,548	548,000	NA	NA	NA	3,350	800,000	628,944
feb	NA	NA	NA	NA	NA	NA	NA	NA	NA
fmc	49,314 a	16,734,865	7,373,664	50,632	18,336,422	8,143,838	51,565	19,954,186	9,261,347
fum	NA	NA	NA	56,605	6,428,458	1,551,036	51,032	6,749,045	1,691,190
ggb	NA	NA	NA	NA	NA	NA	NA	NA	NA
lca	2,166,615	228,081,405	44,531,126	2,183,131	222,637,156	55,646,303	2,187,995	243,449,466	58,761,005
lms	2,010,456	249,150,470	55,076,955	2,018,530	266,546,758	55,896,061	2,026,336	287,098,403	56,831,860
mch	92,390	13,792,266	9,887,051	94,209	15,332,908	11,860,385	93,092	17,215,234	12,259,924
mca	25,583	3,304,388	513,685	25,512	3,567,406	552,512	24,938	4,088,195	573,619
nab	41,437	6,604,693	2,142,148	42,122	7,781,298	2,470,317	42,277	8,902,540	3,302,348
opc	NA	NA	NA	NA	NA	NA	10,372	3,287,612	892,889
pch	3,619,768 a	502,237,350	100,966,089	3,535,825	529,327,006	111,027,318	3,484,985	563,106,353	125,035,379
rca	210,866 a	41,053,364 a	11,470,631 a	212,349 a	44,681,053 a	11,994,379 a	211,628 a	49,083,734 a	13,163,739 a
sda	479,799	67,241,956	166,166,766	495,699	72,060,121	184,689,250	509,792	81,577,130	184,648,454
sbc	12,513,378	1,123,264,849	219,214,770	12,733,124	1,237,594,037	237,452,055	12,917,992	1,382,794,494	262,144,889
ucc	1,841,312	184,292,017	30,243,223	1,818,762	193,524,114	32,125,332	1,801,241	207,486,324	33,862,658
wel	286,858	32,683,492	10,002,869	293,237	35,889,331	11,212,937	297,862	40,017,991	11,300,102
Total	28,144,054	3,113,766,283	790,822,230	28,426,049	3,359,095,603	902,901,429	28,542,929	3,678,586,675	963,445,135

[a]Data obtained from denominational source.

Appendix B-1: Church Member Giving, 1968-1995 (continued)

	Data Year 1977			Data Year 1978			Data Year 1979		
	Full/Confirmed Members	Congregational Finances	Benevolences	Full/Confirmed Members	Congregational Finances	Benevolences	Full/Confirmed Members	Congregational Finances	Benevolences
abc	1,146,084 a	172,710,063	27,765,800	1,008,495 a	184,716,172	31,937,862	1,036,054 a	195,986,995 a	34,992,300
alc	1,772,227	231,960,304	54,085,201	1,773,179	256,371,804	57,145,861	1,768,071	284,019,905	63,903,906
arp	NA	NA	NA	28,644	5,865,416	1,527,561	28,513	6,155,196	1,858,199
bcc	NA	NA	NA	NA	NA	NA	12,923	5,519,037	1,312,046
ccd	817,288	148,880,340	25,698,856	791,633	166,249,455	25,790,367	773,765	172,270,978	27,335,440
cga	171,947	51,969,150	10,001,062	173,753	57,630,848	11,214,530	175,113	65,974,517	12,434,621
cgg	7,595	1,130,000	110,000	7,550	1,135,000	110,000	7,620	1,170,000	105,000
chb	177,534	23,722,817	8,228,903	175,335	25,397,531	9,476,220	172,115	28,422,684	10,161,266
chn	455,100	141,807,024	34,895,751 a	462,124	153,943,138	38,300,431 a	473,726	170,515,940 a	42,087,862 a
ccc	22,171	3,970,337	1,531,645	22,750	4,343,900	1,610,412	23,751	5,054,699	1,849,258
cpc	88,353	11,611,365	1,781,862	88,093	13,657,931	2,136,706	89,218	13,905,745	2,513,625
ecc	28,840	4,860,936	1,132,782	28,712	4,943,032	1,257,777	28,459	5,514,834	1,454,826
ecv	74,060	23,531,176	7,240,548	74,678	26,200,708	8,017,623	76,092	29,987,284	9,400,074
elc	ALC & LCA	ALC & LCA	ALC & LCA	ALC & LCA	ALC & LCA	ALC & LCA	ALC & LCA	ALC & LCA	ALC & LCA
els	14,652	2,290,697	578,390	14,833	2,629,719	839,132	15,081	2,750,703	869,162
emc	NA	NA	NA	3,634	1,281,761	794,896	3,704	1,380,806	828,264
feb	NA	NA	NA	3,956	970,960	745,059	NA	NA	NA
fmc	52,563	22,417,964	10,163,648	55,493	23,911,458	10,121,800	NA	NA	NA
fum	52,599	6,943,990	1,895,984	53,390	8,172,337	1,968,884	51,426	6,662,787	2,131,108
ggb	72,030	9,854,533	747,842	NA	NA	NA	73,046	13,131,345	1,218,763
lca	2,191,942	251,083,883	62,076,894	2,183,666	277,186,563	72,426,148	2,177,231	301,605,382	71,325,097
lms	1,991,408	301,064,630	57,077,162	1,969,279	329,134,237	59,030,753	1,965,422	360,989,735	63,530,596
mch	96,609	18,540,237	12,980,502	97,142	22,922,417	14,070,757	98,027	24,505,346	15,116,762
mca	25,323	4,583,616	581,200	24,854	4,441,750	625,536	24,782	4,600,331	689,070
nab	42,724	10,332,556	3,554,204	42,499	11,629,309	3,559,983	42,779	13,415,024	3,564,339
opc	10,920	3,514,172	931,935	10,939	4,107,705	1,135,388	11,300	4,683,302	1,147,191
pch	3,430,927	633,187,916	130,252,348	3,382,783	692,872,811	128,194,954	3,321,787	776,049,247	148,528,993
rca	210,637 a	53,999,791 a	14,210,966 a	211,778 a	60,138,720 a	15,494,816 a	210,700 a	62,997,526 a	16,750,408 a
sda	522,317	98,468,365	216,202,975	535,705	104,044,989	226,692,736	553,089	118,711,906	255,936,372
sbc	13,078,239	1,506,877,921	289,179,711	13,191,394	1,668,120,760	316,462,385	13,372,757	1,864,213,869	355,885,769
ucc	1,785,652	219,878,772	35,522,221	1,769,104	232,593,033	37,789,958	1,745,533	249,443,032	41,100,583
wel	301,944	44,492,259	11,639,834	303,944	50,255,539	12,960,885	306,264	54,983,467	14,230,208
Total	28,641,685	4,003,684,814	1,020,068,226	28,489,339	4,394,869,003	1,091,439,420	28,638,348	4,844,621,622	1,202,261,108

[a]Data obtained from denominational source.

Appendix B-1: Church Member Giving, 1968-1995 (continued)

	Data Year 1980			Data Year 1981			Data Year 1982		
	Full/Confirmed Members	Congregational Finances	Benevolences	Full/Confirmed Members	Congregational Finances	Benevolences	Full/Confirmed Members	Congregational Finances	Benevolences
abc	1,008,700 [a]	213,560,656	37,133,159	989,322 [a]	227,931,461	40,046,261	983,580 [a]	242,750,027	41,457,745
alc	1,763,067	312,592,610	65,235,739	1,758,452	330,155,588	96,102,638	1,758,239	359,848,865	77,010,444
arp	NA	NA	NA	NA	NA	NA	NA	NA	NA
bcc	NA	NA	NA	13,993	6,781,857	1,740,711	NA	NA	NA
ccd	788,394	189,176,399	30,991,519	772,466	211,828,751	31,067,142	770,227	227,178,861	34,307,638
oga	176,429	67,367,485	13,414,112	178,581	78,322,907	14,907,277	184,685	84,896,806	17,171,600
cgg	NA	NA	NA	5,981	1,788,298	403,000	NA	NA	NA
chb	170,839	29,813,265	11,663,976	170,267	31,641,019	12,929,076	168,844	35,064,568	12,844,415
chn	483,101	191,536,556	45,786,446 [a]	490,852	203,145,992	50,084,163 [a]	497,261	221,947,940	53,232,461 [a]
ccc	NA	NA	NA	25,011	8,465,804	2,415,233	26,008	9,230,111	2,574,569
cpc	90,844	16,448,164	2,835,695	91,665	17,225,308	3,504,763	91,774	18,600,022	2,703,521
ecc	27,995	6,043,687	1,517,857	27,567	6,043,687	1,724,722	27,405	6,888,607	1,734,914
ecv	77,737	33,191,322	10,031,072	79,523	37,884,792	8,689,918	81,324	42,599,609	8,830,793
elc	ALC & LCA	ALC & LCA	ALC & LCA	ALC & LCA	ALC & LCA	ALC & LCA	ALC & LCA	ALC & LCA	ALC & LCA
els	14,968	3,154,804	851,308	14,904	3,461,387	716,624	15,165	3,767,977	804,822
emc	3,782	1,527,945	1,041,447	3,753	1,515,975	908,342	3,832	1,985,890	731,510
feb	4,329	1,250,466	627,536	NA	NA	NA	2,047	696,660	1,020,972
fmc	NA	NA	NA	NA	NA	NA	54,198	35,056,434	8,051,593
fum	51,691	9,437,724	2,328,137	51,248	9,551,765	2,449,731	50,601	10,334,180	2,597,215
ggb	74,159	14,967,312	1,547,038	75,028	15,816,060	1,473,070	NA	NA	NA
lca	2,176,991	371,981,816	87,439,137	2,173,558	404,300,509	82,862,299	2,176,265	435,564,519	83,217,264
lms	1,973,958	390,756,268	66,626,364	1,983,198	429,910,406	86,341,102	1,961,260	468,468,156	75,457,846
mch	99,511	28,846,931	16,437,738	99,651	31,304,278	17,448,024	101,501	33,583,338	17,981,274
mca	24,863	5,178,444	860,399	24,500	5,675,495	831,177	24,669	6,049,857	812,015
nab	43,041	12,453,858	3,972,485	43,146	15,513,286	4,420,403	42,735	17,302,952	4,597,515
opc	11,550	5,235,294	1,235,849	11,889	5,939,983	1,382,451	NA	NA	NA
pch	3,262,086	820,218,732	176,172,729	3,202,392	896,641,430	188,576,382	3,157,372	970,223,947	199,331,832
rca	210,762	70,733,297	17,313,239 [a]	210,312	77,044,709	18,193,793 [a]	211,168	82,656,050	19,418,165 [a]
sda	571,141	121,484,768	275,783,385	588,536	133,088,131	297,838,046	606,310	136,877,455	299,437,917
sbc	13,600,126	2,080,375,258	400,976,072	13,782,644	2,336,062,506	443,931,179	13,991,709	2,628,272,553	486,402,607
ucc	1,736,244	278,546,571	44,042,186	1,726,535	300,730,591	48,329,399	1,708,847	323,725,191	52,738,069
wel	308,620	60,624,862	16,037,844	311,351	68,056,396	18,261,099	312,195	71,891,457 [a]	18,677,343
Total	28,754,928	5,336,504,494	1,331,902,468	28,906,325	5,895,828,371	1,477,578,025	29,009,221	6,475,462,032	1,523,146,059

[a]Data obtained from denominational source.

Appendix B-1: Church Member Giving, 1968-1995 (continued)

	Data Year 1983			Data Year 1984			Data Year 1985		
	Full/Confirmed Members	Congregational Finances	Benevolences	Full/Confirmed Members	Congregational Finances	Benevolences	Full/Confirmed Members	Congregational Finances	Benevolences
abc	965,117 [a]	254,716,036	43,683,021	953,945 [a]	267,556,088	46,232,040	894,732 [a]	267,694,684	47,201,119 [a]
alc	1,756,420	375,500,188	84,633,617	1,756,558	413,876,101	86,601,067	1,751,649	428,861,660	87,152,699
arp	31,738	9,695,273 [d]	3,125,007 [d]	31,355	11,163,583	2,833,349	32,051	11,839,577	3,360,285
bcc	14,782	7,638,413	1,858,632	15,128	8,160,359	2,586,843	15,535 [a]	8,504,354 [a]	2,979,046 [a]
ccd	761,629	241,934,972	35,809,331	755,233	263,694,210	38,402,791	743,486	274,072,301	40,992,053
cga	182,190	81,309,323	13,896,753	185,404	86,611,269	14,347,570	185,593	91,078,512	15,308,954
cgg	5,759	1,981,300	412,000	4,711	2,211,800	504,200	4,575	2,428,730	582,411
chb	164,680	39,726,743	14,488,192	161,824	37,743,527	15,136,600	159,184	40,658,904	16,509,718
chn	506,439	237,220,642 [a]	57,267,073 [a]	514,937	253,566,280	60,909,810 [a]	520,741	267,134,078	65,627,515 [a]
ccc	26,765	9,197,521	2,980,636	28,383	10,018,982	3,051,425	28,624	11,729,365	3,350,021
cpc	93,387	20,206,646	2,604,569	92,242	21,185,481	3,843,056	85,346 [a]	21,241,302 [a]	3,227,932 [a]
ecc	27,203	7,196,283	1,891,486	26,775	7,380,179	2,019,373	26,016	6,147,413	1,777,172
ecv	82,943	46,397,734	10,615,909	84,185	51,613,393	11,243,908	85,150	54,719,309	13,828,030
elc	ALC & LCA	ALC & LCA	ALC & LCA	ALC & LCA	ALC & LCA	ALC & LCA	ALC & LCA	ALC & LCA	ALC & LCA
els	15,576	3,842,625	838,788	15,396	4,647,714	864,714	15,012	4,725,783	791,586
emc	3,857	1,930,689	738,194	3,908	2,017,565	862,350	3,813	2,128,019	1,058,040
feb	2,094	622,467	1,466,399	NA	NA	NA	2,107 [a]	1,069,851	402,611 [a]
fmc	NA	NA	NA	NA	NA	NA	56,242	42,046,626 [a]	9,461,369 [a]
fum	49,441	11,723,240	2,886,931	48,713	11,549,163	2,875,370	48,812	12,601,820	3,012,658
ggb	75,133	17,283,259	1,733,755	75,028	17,599,169	1,729,228	73,040	18,516,252	1,683,130
lca	2,176,772	457,239,780	88,909,363	2,168,594	496,228,216	99,833,067	2,161,216	539,142,069	103,534,375
lms	1,984,199	499,220,552	97,293,050	1,986,392	539,346,935	104,393,798	1,982,753	566,507,516	105,191,123
mch	110,294	34,153,628	17,581,878	90,347	37,333,306	16,944,094	91,167	34,015,200	25,593,500
mca	24,913	6,618,339	911,787	24,269	7,723,611	1,183,741	24,396	8,698,949	1,170,349
nab	43,286	18,010,853	5,132,672	43,215	19,322,720	5,724,552	42,863	20,246,236	5,766,686
opc	12,045	6,874,722	1,755,169	12,239	7,555,006	2,079,924	12,634	8,291,483	2,204,998
pch	3,122,213	1,047,756,995	197,981,080	3,092,151	1,132,098,779	218,412,639	3,057,226 [a]	1,252,885,684 [a]	232,487,569 [a]
rca	211,660	92,071,986	20,632,574 [a]	209,968 [a]	100,378,778	21,794,880	209,395	103,428,950	22,233,299
sda	623,563	143,636,140	323,461,439	638,929	155,257,063	319,664,449	651,594	155,077,180	346,251,406
sbc	14,178,051	2,838,573,815	528,781,000	14,341,822	3,094,913,877	567,467,188	14,477,364	3,272,276,486	609,868,694
ucc	1,701,513	332,613,396	55,716,557	1,696,107	385,786,198	58,679,094	1,683,777	409,543,989	62,169,679 [a]
wel	313,883	76,133,614 [a]	24,169,441	315,466	82,884,471 [a]	22,951,699	316,297 [a]	87,194,889	22,376,423 [a]
Total	29,267,545	6,921,027,174	1,643,256,303	29,373,224	7,529,423,823	1,733,172,819	29,442,390	8,024,507,171	1,857,154,450

[a]Data obtained from denominational source.

[d]The amounts for Associate Reformed Presbyterian Congregational Finances and Benevolences appear above in reverse order from that presented in the YACC, based on a comparison with other data years.

Appendix B-1: Church Member Giving, 1968-1995 (continued)

	Data Year 1986			Data Year 1987			Data Year 1988		
	Full/Confirmed Members	Congregational Finances	Benevolences	Full/Confirmed Members	Congregational Finances	Benevolences	Full/Confirmed Members	Congregational Finances	Benevolences
abc	862,582 a	287,020,378 a	49,070,083 a	868,189 a	291,606,418 a	55,613,855	825,102 a	296,569,316 e	55,876,771 a
alc	1,740,439	434,641,736	96,147,129	See ELCA	See ELCA	See ELCA	See ELCA	See ELCA	See ELCA
arp	NA	NA	NA	32,289	12,138,959	5,287,424	31,922	13,590,006	5,130,806
bcc	15,911	10,533,883	2,463,558	16,136	11,203,321	3,139,949	NA	NA	NA
ccd	732,466	288,277,386	42,027,504	718,522	287,464,332	42,728,826	707,985	297,187,996	42,226,128
oga	188,662	91,768,855	16,136,647	198,552	124,376,413	20,261,687	198,842	132,384,232	19,781,941
cgg	NA	NA	NA	4,348	2,437,778	738,818	NA	NA	NA
chb	155,967	43,531,293	17,859,101	154,067	45,201,732	19,342,402	151,169	48,008,657	19,701,942 a
chn	529,192	283,189,977	68,438,998 a	541,878	294,160,356	73,033,568	550,700	309,478,442	74,737,057 a
ccc	28,948	15,646,859	3,961,037	29,429	15,509,349	3,740,688	29,015	13,853,547	4,120,974
cpc	91,556	22,992,625	3,782,282	85,781	22,857,711	3,727,681	85,304	23,366,911 e	3,722,607
ecc	25,625	8,619,708	1,399,871	25,300	8,689,978	2,436,473	24,980	12,115,762	2,742,873
ecv	86,079	57,628,572	14,374,707	86,741	61,049,703	14,636,000	87,750	64,920,459	14,471,178
elc	ALC & LCA	ALC & LCA	ALC & LCA	3,952,663	1,083,293,684	169,685,942	3,931,878	1,150,483,034	169,580,472
els	15,082	4,941,917	1,028,974	15,892	5,298,882	1,082,198	NA	NA	NA
emc	NA	NA	NA	3,841	2,332,216	1,326,711	3,879	2,522,533	1,438,459
feb	NA	NA	NA	NA	NA	NA	NA	NA	NA
fmc	56,243	46,150,881	9,446,120	57,262	47,743,298	9,938,096	57,432	48,788,041	9,952,103
fum	48,143	12,790,909	2,916,870	47,173	13,768,272	3,631,353	48,325	14,127,491	3,719,125
ggb	72,263	19,743,265	1,883,826	73,515	20,850,827	1,789,578	74,086	21,218,051	1,731,299
lca	2,157,701	569,250,519	111,871,174	See ELCA	See ELCA	See ELCA	See ELCA	See ELCA	See ELCA
lms	1,974,798	605,768,688	111,938,197	1,973,347	620,271,274	109,681,025	1,962,674	659,288,332	112,694,841
mch	NA	NA	NA	92,902	43,295,100	25,033,600	92,682	47,771,200	27,043,900
mca	24,260	8,133,127	1,155,350	24,440	9,590,658	1,174,593	23,526	9,221,646	1,210,476
nab	42,084	20,961,799	5,982,391	13,301	9,884,288	NA	42,629	24,597,288	6,611,840
opc	NA	NA	NA	NA	NA	2,425,480	NA	NA	NA
pch	3,007,322	1,318,440,264	249,033,881	2,967,781	1,395,501,073	247,234,439	2,929,608	1,439,655,217	284,989,138
rca	207,993	114,231,429	22,954,596	203,581	114,652,192 a	24,043,270	200,631	127,409,263	25,496,802 a
sda	666,199	166,692,974	361,316,753	675,702	166,939,355	374,830,065	687,200	178,768,967	395,849,223
sbc	14,613,638	3,481,124,471	635,196,984	14,722,617	3,629,842,643	662,455,177	14,812,844	3,706,652,161	689,366,904
ucc	1,676,105	429,340,239	63,808,091	1,662,568	451,700,210	66,870,922	1,644,787	470,747,740	65,734,348
wel	316,416	92,662,969 a	22,448,920	317,294	97,567,101 a	22,207,123	316,987	101,975,092 a	22,406,238
Total	29,335,674	8,434,084,723	1,916,643,044	29,565,111	8,889,227,123	1,968,096,943	29,521,937	9,214,701,384	2,060,337,445

[a]Data obtained from denominational source.

[e]A YACC prepublication data table listed 23,366,911 for Congregational Finances which, added to Benevolences, equals the published Total of 27,089,518.

Appendix B-1: Church Member Giving, 1968-1995 (continued)

	Data Year 1989			Data Year 1990			Data Year 1991		
	Full/Confirmed Members	Congregational Finances	Benevolences	Full/Confirmed Members	Congregational Finances	Benevolences	Full/Confirmed Members	Congregational Finances	Benevolences
abc	789,730 [a]	305,212,094 [a]	55,951,539	764,890 [a]	315,777,005 [a]	54,740,278	773,838 [a]	318,150,548 [a]	52,330,924 [a]
alc	See ELCA	See ELCA	See ELCA	See ELCA	See ELCA	See ELCA	See ELCA	See ELCA	See ELCA
arp	32,600	15,030,209	5,390,867	32,787	16,666,990	5,317,162	33,494	16,932,998 [a]	5,907,013 [a]
bcc	16,842	12,840,038	3,370,306	17,277	13,327,414	3,336,580	17,456	14,491,918 [a]	3,294,169 [a]
ccd	690,115	310,043,826	42,015,246	678,750	321,569,909	42,607,007	663,336	331,629,009	43,339,307
cga	199,786	134,918,052	20,215,075	205,884	141,375,027	21,087,504	214,743	146,249,447 [a]	21,801,570 [a]
cgg	4,415	3,367,000	686,000	4,399	3,106,729	690,000	4,375	2,756,651	662,500
chb	149,681	51,921,820	19,737,714 [a]	148,253	54,832,226	18,384,483 [a]	147,954 [a]	55,035,355 [a]	19,694,919 [a]
chn	558,664	322,924,598	76,625,913 [a]	563,756 [a]	333,397,255 [a]	77,991,665 [a]	572,153	352,654,251	82,276,097 [a]
ccc	28,413	18,199,823	4,064,111	28,355	16,964,128	4,174,133	28,035	17,760,290	4,304,052
cpc	84,866	25,326,430	4,092,869	91,857	28,364,344	4,355,823	91,650 [a]	29,442,581 [a]	5,972,155 [a]
ecc	24,606	10,328,892	2,676,388	24,437	9,946,582	2,442,778	24,383	10,452,528 [a]	3,075,773 [a]
ecv	89,014	66,585,214	15,206,265	89,735	70,568,800	15,601,475	89,648	74,154,515	16,598,656
elc	3,909,302	1,239,433,257	182,386,940	3,898,478	1,318,884,279	184,174,554	3,890,947	1,375,439,787	186,016,168
els	15,740	6,186,648	1,342,321	16,181	6,527,076	1,193,789	16,004	6,657,338	1,030,445
emc	3,888	2,712,843	1,567,728	4,026	2,991,485	1,800,593	3,958	3,394,563	1,790,115
feb	NA	NA	NA	NA	NA	NA	2,008 [a]	1,398,968	500,092 [a]
fmc	59,418 [a]	50,114,090 [a]	10,311,535 [a]	58,084	55,229,181	10,118,505	57,794	57,880,464	9,876,739
fum	47,228	16,288,644	4,055,624	45,691	10,036,083	2,511,063	NA	NA	NA
ggb	73,738	23,127,835	1,768,804	74,156	23,127,835	1,737,011	71,119 [a]	22,362,874 [a]	1,408,262 [a]
lca	See ELCA	See ELCA	See ELCA	See ELCA	See ELCA	See ELCA	See ELCA	See ELCA	See ELCA
lms	1,961,114	701,701,168 [a]	118,511,582 [a]	1,954,350	712,235,204	129,229,080	1,952,845	741,823,412	124,932,427
mch	92,517	55,353,313	27,873,241	96,487 [a]	65,709,827	28,397,083	99,431	68,926,324	28,464,199
mca	23,802	10,415,640	1,284,233	23,526	10,105,037	1,337,616	22,887	10,095,337	1,205,335
nab	42,629	28,076,077	3,890,017	44,493	31,103,672	7,700,119	43,187 [a]	27,335,239 [a]	7,792,876 [a]
opc	NA	NA	NA	NA	NA	NA	12,265	11,700,000	2,700,000
pch	2,886,482	1,528,450,805	295,365,032	2,847,437	1,530,341,707	294,990,441	2,805,548	1,636,407,042 [a]	311,905,934 [a]
rca	198,832	136,796,188 [a]	29,456,132 [a]	197,154	144,357,953 [a]	27,705,029	193,531	147,532,382 [a]	26,821,721 [a]
sda	701,781	196,204,538	415,752,350	717,446	195,054,218	433,035,080	733,026	201,411,183	456,242,995
sbc	14,907,826	3,873,300,782	712,738,838	15,038,409	4,146,285,561	718,174,874	15,232,347	4,283,283,059	731,812,766
ucc	1,625,969	496,825,160	72,300,698	1,599,212	527,378,397	71,984,897	1,583,830	543,803,752	73,149,887
wel	317,117	110,575,539 [a]	22,811,571	316,813	116,272,092 [a]	24,088,568	316,929 [a]	121,835,547 [a]	24,276,370 [a]
Total	29,536,115	9,752,260,523	2,151,448,939	29,582,323	10,221,536,016	2,188,907,190	29,698,721	10,630,997,362	2,249,183,466

[a]Data obtained from denominational source.

Appendix B-1: Church Member Giving, 1968-1995 (continued)

	Data Year 1992			Data Year 1993			Data Year 1994		
	Full/Confirmed Members	Congregational Finances	Benevolences	Full/Confirmed Members	Congregational Finances	Benevolences	Full/Confirmed Members	Congregational Finances	Benevolences
abc	730,009 a	310,307,040 a	52,764,005 a	764,657 a	346,658,047 a	53,562,811 a	697,379 a	337,185,885 a	51,553,256 a
alc	See ELCA	See ELCA	See ELCA	See ELCA	See ELCA	See ELCA	See ELCA	See ELCA	See ELCA
arp	33,550	16,671,405 a	6,988,560 a	33,662 a	18,268,493 a	5,822,845 a	33,636	20,897,526	6,727,857
bcc	17,646 a	15,981,118 a	3,159,717 a	17,986	13,786,394	4,515,730 a	18,152	14,844,672	5,622,005
ccd	655,652	333,629,412	46,440,333	619,028	328,219,027	44,790,415	605,996	342,352,080	43,165,285
cga	214,743	150,115,497	23,500,213	216,117	158,454,703	23,620,177	221,346 a	160,694,760 a	26,262,049 a
cgg	4,085	2,648,085	509,398	4,239	2,793,000	587,705	3,996	2,934,843	475,799
chb	147,912	57,954,895	21,748,320	146,713	56,818,998	23,278,848	144,282	57,210,682	24,155,595
chn	582,804 a	361,555,793 a	84,118,580 a	589,398	369,896,767	87,416,378 a	595,303	387,385,034	89,721,860
ccc	30,387	22,979,946	4,311,234	36,864	23,736,161	5,272,184	37,996 a	23,758,101 a	5,240,805 a
cpc	92,240 a	29,721,914 a	4,588,604 a	91,489	29,430,921	4,852,663	90,125	31,732,121	4,864,472
ecc	24,150 a	11,180,607 a	3,086,730 a	23,889	11,397,710	3,259,095	23,504	13,931,409	3,269,986
ecv	90,985 a	75,806,590 a	16,732,701 a	89,511	79,741,500	16,482,315	90,919 a	86,043,313 a	17,874,955 a
elc	3,878,055 a	1,399,419,800	189,605,837 a	3,861,418	1,452,000,815	188,393,158	3,849,692 a	1,502,746,601	187,145,886
els	15,929 a	6,944,522 a	1,271,058 a	15,780	6,759,222 a	1,100,660	15,960	7,288,521	1,195,698
emc	4,059 a	3,834,001	2,299,864	4,130 a	4,260,307 a	1,406,682 a	4,225 a	4,597,730 a	1,533,157 a
feb	1,872 a	1,343,225 a	397,553 a	1,866 a	1,294,646 a	429,023 a	1,898 a	1,537,041 a	395,719 a
fmc	58,220 a	60,584,079	10,591,064	59,156	62,478,294	10,513,187	59,354 a	65,359,325 a	10,708,854 a
fum	NA	NA	NA	NA	NA	NA	NA	NA	NA
ggb	72,388 a	21,561,432 a	1,402,330 a	73,129 a	22,376,970 a	1,440,342 a	71,140 a	19,651,624 a	2,052,409 a
lca	See ELCA	See ELCA	See ELCA	See ELCA	See ELCA	See ELCA	See ELCA	See ELCA	See ELCA
lms	1,953,248	777,467,488	131,684,905	1,945,077	789,821,559	130,761,788	1,944,905	817,412,113	129,525,358
mch	99,446	68,118,222	28,835,719	95,634	71,385,271	27,973,380	87,911 a	64,651,639	24,830,192
mca	22,533	10,150,953	1,208,372	22,223	9,675,502	1,191,131	21,448	9,753,010	1,182,778
nab	43,446	28,375,947	7,327,594	43,045	30,676,902	7,454,087	43,236	32,800,560	7,515,707
opc	12,580 a	12,466,266 a	3,025,824 a	12,924 a	13,158,089 a	3,039,676 a	13,970	14,393,880	3,120,454
pch	2,780,406	1,696,092,968	309,069,530	2,742,192	1,700,918,712	310,375,024	2,698,262	1,800,008,292	307,158,749
rca	190,322 a	147,181,320 a	28,457,900 a	188,551 a	159,715,941 a	26,009,853 a	185,242	153,107,408	27,906,830
sda	748,687	191,362,737	476,902,779	761,703	209,524,570	473,769,831	775,349	229,596,444	503,347,816
sbc	15,358,866	4,462,915,112	751,366,698	15,398,642	4,621,157,751	761,298,249	15,614,060	4,915,453,127 a	809,966,842 a
ucc	1,555,382	521,190,413	73,906,372	1,530,178	550,847,702	71,046,517	1,501,310	556,540,722	67,269,762
wel	316,183 a	127,858,970 a	26,426,128 a	315,871	137,187,582	24,587,988	315,302	142,851,919	23,998,935
Total	29,735,785	10,925,419,757	2,311,727,922	29,705,072	11,282,441,556	2,314,251,742	29,765,898	11,816,720,382	2,387,789,070

[a] Data obtained from denominational source.

Note: Data in italics indicates a change from the previous edition in the series.

Appendix B-1: Church Member Giving, 1968-1995 (continued)

Data Year 1995

	Full/Confirmed Members	Congregational Finances	Benevolences
abc	726,452 [a]	365,873,197 [a]	57,052,333 [a]
alc	See ELCA	See ELCA	See ELCA
arp	33,513	21,485,535 [a]	5,711,882 [a]
boc	18,529	16,032,149	5,480,828
ccd	601,237	357,895,652	42,887,958
cga	224,061	160,897,147	26,192,559
cgg	3,877	2,722,766	486,661
chb	143,121	60,242,418	22,599,214
chn	598,946	396,698,137	93,440,095
ccc	38,853 [a]	24,250,819 [a]	5,483,659 [a]
cpc	87,896	33,535,975	5,051,095
ecc	23,422	14,830,454	3,301,060
ecv	91,458	92,970,066	17,565,085
elc	3,845,063	1,551,842,465	188,107,066
els	16,543	13,112,485	1,084,136
emc	4,284 [a]	5,694,325 [a]	1,230,302 [a]
feb	1,856 [a]	1,412,281 [a]	447,544 [a]
fmc	59,060	67,687,955	11,114,804
fum	NA	NA	NA
ggb	70,886 [a]	24,385,956 [a]	1,722,662 [a]
lca	See ELCA	See ELCA	See ELCA
lms	1,943,281	832,701,255	130,511,413
mch	90,812	71,641,773	26,832,240
mca	21,409	10,996,031	1,167,513
nab	43,928	37,078,473	7,480,331
opc	14,355	16,017,003	3,376,691
pch	2,665,276	1,855,684,719	309,978,224
rca	183,255	164,250,624	29,995,068
sda	790,731	240,565,576	503,334,129
sbc	15,663,296	5,209,748,503	858,635,435
ucc	1,472,213	578,042,965	67,806,448
wel	314,169	150,839,040	35,191,390
Total	29,791,782	12,379,135,744	2,463,267,825

[a]Data obtained from denominational source.

Note: Data in italics indicates a change from the previous edition in the series.

Appendix B-2: Church Member Giving for 49 Denominations, 1994-1995

	Data Year 1994			Data Year 1995		
	Full/Confirmed Members	Congregational Finances	Benevolences	Full/Confirmed Members	Congregational Finances	Benevolences
Albanian Orthodox Diocese of America	1,875	161,000	18,100	1,984	167,500	15,600
Allegheny Wesleyan Methodist Connection (Original Allegheny Conference)	1,905	3,500,213	954,931	1,899	3,225,087	942,938
Apostolic Faith Mission Church of God	8,000	196,000	262,000	8,400	206,000	273,000
Baptist Missionary Association of America	230,171	50,782,987	10,782,987	231,191	52,609,191	10,198,727
Christian and Missionary Alliance	147,560 [a]	170,376,194 [a]	36,407,346 [a]	147,955	177,875,082	40,576,052
Church of Lutheran Brethren of America	8,331	7,275,256	1,890,818	8,114	6,697,904	2,459,460
Church of the Lutheran Confession	6,510	3,222,816	672,173	6,474	3,975,789	3,276,827
Churches of God General Conference	31,862	15,716,667	3,295,868	31,745	16,822,826	3,637,695
The Episcopal Church	1,577,996 [a]	1,444,416,489 [a]	252,242,370 [a]	1,585,930	1,565,904,844	256,555,466
The Evangelical Church	12,458	9,037,809	2,383,583	12,444	9,004,206	2,565,297
General Conf. Mennonite Brethren Church	19,218	24,739,016	7,547,727	18,240	25,037,110	7,573,206
International Pentecostal Church of Christ	2,668	2,298,803	1,480,862	2,311	2,215,078	1,836,821
International Pentecostal Holiness Church	150,133	3,637,135	6,037,676	157,163	3,662,681	6,534,372
The Latvian Evangelical Lutheran Church in America	11,322	3,246,474	442,618	10,970	3,004,427	453,947
Missionary Church, Inc.	28,821	34,679,795 [a]	7,068,428	29,542	38,085,125	7,403,580
Primitive Methodist Church in the U.S.A.	5,216 [a]	4,377,247 [a]	5,619,446 [a]	5,130	4,305,211	4,869,635
The Schwenkfelder Church	2,577	898,946	183,974	2,524	973,300	183,586
United Brethren in Christ	24,671	15,422,774	2,986,983	24,095	16,567,272	3,092,056
The United Methodist Church	8,584,125	2,698,513,430	731,838,348	8,538,662	2,825,235,543	743,304,674
The Wesleyan Church	109,694	118,843,931	23,435,980	109,150	126,917,905	29,232,828

[a] Data obtained from denominational source.

Appendix B-3.1: Church Member Giving for Eleven Denominations, 1921-1952, in Current Dollars

Year	Total Contributions	Members	Per Capita Giving
1921	$281,173,263	17,459,611	$16.10
1922	345,995,802	18,257,426	18.95
1923	415,556,876	18,866,775	22.03
1924	443,187,826	19,245,220	23.03
1925	412,658,363	19,474,863	21.19
1926	368,529,223	17,054,404	21.61
1927	459,527,624	20,266,709	22.67
1928	429,947,883	20,910,584	20.56
1929	445,327,233	20,612,910	21.60
1930	419,697,819	20,796,745	20.18
1931	367,158,877	21,508,745	17.07
1932	309,409,873	21,757,411	14.22
1933	260,366,681	21,792,663	11.95
1934	260,681,472	22,105,624	11.79
1935	267,596,925	22,204,355	12.05
1936	279,835,526	21,746,023	12.87
1937	297,134,313	21,906,456	13.56
1938	307,217,666	22,330,090	13.76
1939	302,300,476	23,084,048	13.10
1940	311,362,429	23,671,660	13.15
1941	336,732,622	23,120,929	14.56
1942	358,419,893	23,556,204	15.22
1943	400,742,492	24,679,784	16.24
1944	461,500,396	25,217,319	18.30
1945	551,404,448	25,898,642	21.29
1946	608,165,179	26,158,559	23.25
1947	684,393,895	27,082,905	25.27
1948	775,360,993	27,036,992	28.68
1949	875,069,944	27,611,824	31.69
1950	934,723,015	28,176,095	33.17
1951	1,033,391,527	28,974,314	35.67
1952	1,121,802,639	29,304,909	38.28

Appendix B-3.2: Church Member Giving for Eleven Denominations, 1953-1967

	Data Year 1953		Data Year 1954		Data Year 1955	
	Total Contributions	Per Capita Total Contributions	Total Contributions	Per Capita Total Contributions	Total Contributions	Per Capita Total Contributions
American Baptist (Northern)	$66,557,447 [a]	$44.50 [b]	$65,354,184	$43.17	$67,538,753 [d]	$44.19
Christian Ch (Disciples of Christ)	$60,065,545 [c]	$32.50 [b]	$65,925,164	$34.77	$68,611,162 [d]	$35.96
Church of the Brethren	$7,458,584	$43.78	$7,812,806	$45.88	$9,130,616	$53.00
The Episcopal Church	$84,209,027	$49.02	$92,079,668	$51.84	$97,541,567 [d]	$50.94 [b]
Evangelical Lutheran Church in Am.						
The American Lutheran Church						
American Lutheran Church	$30,881,256	$55.24	$34,202,987	$58.83	$40,411,856	$67.03
The Evangelical Lutheran Church	$30,313,907	$48.70	$33,312,926	$51.64	$37,070,341	$55.29
United Evangelical Lutheran Ch.	$1,953,163	$55.85	$2,268,200	$50.25	$2,635,469	$69.84
Lutheran Free Church	Not Reported: YACC 1955, p. 264		$2,101,026	$44.51	$2,708,747	$55.76
Evan. Lutheran Churches, Assn of	Not Reported: YACC 1955, p. 264		Not Reported: YACC 1956, p. 276		Not Reported: YACC 1957, p. 284	
Lutheran Church in America						
United Lutheran Church	$67,721,548	$45.68	$76,304,344	$50.25	$83,170,787	$53.46
General Council Evang Luth Ch						
General Synod of Evan Luth Ch						
United Syn Evang Luth. South						
American Evangelical Luth. Ch	Not Reported: YACC 1955, p. 264		Not Reported: YACC 1956, p. 276		Not Reported: YACC 1957, p. 284	
Augustana Lutheran Church	$18,733,019	$53.98	$22,203,098	$62.14	$22,090,350	$60.12
Finnish Luth. Ch (Suomi Synod)	$744,971	$32.12	$674,554	$29.47	$1,059,682	$43.75
Moravian Church in Am. No. Prov.	$1,235,534	$53.26	$1,461,658	$59.51	$1,241,008	$49.15
Presbyterian Church (U.S.A.)						
United Presbyterian Ch in U.S.A.						
Presbyterian Ch in the U.S.A.	$141,057,179	$56.49	$158,110,613	$61.47	$180,472,698	$68.09
United Presbyterian Ch in N.A.	$13,204,897	$57.73	$14,797,353	$62.37	$16,019,616	$65.39
Presbyterian Church in the U.S.	$56,001,996	$73.99	$59,222,983	$75.54	$66,033,260	$81.43
Reformed Church in America	$13,671,897	$68.57	$14,740,275	$71.87	$17,459,572	$84.05
Southern Baptist Convention	$278,851,129	$39.84	$305,573,654	$42.17	$334,836,283	$44.54
United Church of Christ						
Congregational Christian	$64,061,866	$49.91	$71,786,834	$54.76	$80,519,810	$60.00
Congregational						
Evangelical and Reformed	$31,025,133	$41.24	$36,261,267	$46.83	$41,363,406	$52.74
Evangelical Synod of N.A./German Reformed Church in the U.S.						
The United Methodist Church						
The Evangelical United Brethren	$36,331,994	$50.21	$36,609,598	$50.43	$41,199,631	$56.01
The Methodist Church	$314,521,214	$34.37	$345,416,448	$37.53	$389,490,613	$41.82
Methodist Episcopal Church						
Methodist Episcopal Ch South						
Methodist Protestant Church						
Total	$1,318,601,306		$1,446,219,640		$1,600,655,226	

[a] In data year 1953, $805,135 has been subtracted from the 1955 Yearbook of American Churches (Edition for 1956) entry. See 1956 Yearbook of American Church for 1957), p. 276, n.1.

[b] To obtain comparable membership figures in order to calculate giving as a percentage of income based on the revised Total Contributions data, the Total Contributions figure as published in the Yearbook was divided by the published per capita figure yielding a membership figure. The revised Total Contributions figure was then divided by the total calculated membership to obtain the revised per capita figure included in the above table.

[c] In data year 1953, $5,508,883 has been added to the 1955 Yearbook of American Churches (Edition for 1956) entry. See 1956 Yearbook of American Churches (Edition for 1957), p. 276, n. 4.

[d] Total Contributions averaged from available data as follows: The Episcopal Church, 1954 and 1956 data; American Baptist Churches, 1954 and 1957 data; Christian (Disiples of Christ), 1954 and 1956 data.

Appendix B-3.2: Church Member Giving for Eleven Denominations, 1953-1967 (continued)

	Data Year 1956		Data Year 1957		Data Year 1958	
	Total Contributions	Per Capita Total Contributions	Total Contributions	Per Capita Total Contributions	Total Contributions	Per Capita Total Contributions
American Baptist (Northern)	$69,723,321 d	$45.21	$71,907,890	$46.23	$70,405,404	$45.03
Christian Ch (Disciples of Christ)	$71,397,159	$37.14	$73,737,955	$37.94	$79,127,458	$41.17
Church of the Brethren	$10,936,285	$63.15	$11,293,388	$64.43	$12,288,049	$70.03
The Episcopal Church	$103,003,465	$52.79	$111,660,728	$53.48	$120,687,177	$58.33
Evangelical Lutheran Church in Am.						
The American Lutheran Church						
American Lutheran Church	$45,316,809	$72.35	$44,518,194	$68.80	$47,216,896	$70.89
The Evangelical Lutheran Church	$39,096,038	$56.47	$44,212,046	$61.95	$45,366,512	$61.74
United Evangelical Lutheran Ch.	$2,843,527	$73.57	$2,641,201	$65.46	$3,256,050	$77.38
Lutheran Free Church	$2,652,307	$53.14	$3,379,882	$64.70	$3,519,017	$66.31
Evan. Lutheran Churches, Assn of	Not Reported: YACC 1958, p. 292		Not Reported: YACC 1959, p. 277		Not Reported: YACC 1960, p. 276	
Lutheran Church in America						
United Lutheran Church	$93,321,223	$58.46	$100,943,860	$61.89	$110,179,054	$66.45
General Council Evang Luth Ch						
General Synod of Evan Luth Ch						
United Syn Evang Luth South						
American Evangelical Luth. Ch	Not Comparable (YACC 1958, p. 292)		$935,319	$59.45	$1,167,503	$72.98
Augustana Lutheran Church	$24,893,792	$66.15	$28,180,152	$72.09	$29,163,771	$73.17
Finnish Luth. Ch (Suomi Synod)	$1,308,026	$51.56	$1,524,299	$58.11	$1,533,058	$61.94
Moravian Church in Am. No. Prov.	$1,740,961	$67.53	$1,776,703	$67.77	$1,816,281	$68.14
Presbyterian Church (U.S.A.)						
United Presbyterian Ch in the U.S.A.					$243,000,572	$78.29
Presbyterian Ch in the U.S.A.	$204,208,085	$75.02	$214,253,598	$77.06		
United Presbyterian Ch in N.A.	$18,424,936	$73.30	$19,117,837	$74.24		
Presbyterian Church in the U.S.	$73,477,555	$88.56	$78,426,424	$92.03	$82,760,291	$95.18
Reformed Church in America	$18,718,008	$88.56	$19,658,604	$91.10	$21,550,017	$98.24
Southern Baptist Convention	$372,136,675	$48.17	$397,540,347	$49.99	$419,619,438	$51.04
United Church of Christ						
Congregational Christian	$89,914,505	$65.18	$90,333,453	$64.87	$97,480,446	$69.55
Congregational						
Evangelical and Reformed	$51,519,531	$64.88	$55,718,141	$69.56	$63,419,468	$78.56
Evangelical Synod of N.A./German						
Reformed Church in the U.S.						
The United Methodist Church						
The Evangelical United Brethren	$44,727,060	$60.57	$45,738,332 d	$61.75	$46,749,605 d	$62.93
The Methodist Church	$413,893,955	$43.82	$462,826,269 d	$48.31	$511,758,582	$52.80
Methodist Episcopal Church						
Methodist Episcopal Ch South						
Methodist Protestant Church						
Total	$1,753,253,223		$1,880,324,622		$2,012,064,649	

d Total Contributions averaged from available data as follows: 1956 American Baptist Churches, 1954 and 1957 data; 1957 and 1958 Evangelical United Brethren, 1956 and 1960 data; 1957 The Methodist Church, 1956 and 1958 data.

Appendix B-3.2: Church member Giving for Eleven Denominations, 1953-1967 (continued)

	Data Year 1959 Total Contributions	Per Capita Total Contributions	Data Year 1960 Total Contributions	Per Capita Total Contributions	Data Year 1961 Total Contributions	Per Capita Total Contributions
American Baptist (Northern)	$74,877,669	$48.52	$73,106,232	$48.06	$104,887,025	$68.96
Christian Ch (Disciples of Christ)	$84,375,152 d	$51.22	$86,834,944	$63.26	$89,730,589	$65.31
Church of the Brethren	$12,143,983	$65.27	$12,644,194	$68.33	$13,653,155	$73.33
The Episcopal Church	$130,279,752	$61.36	$140,625,284	$64.51	$154,458,809	$68.30
Evangelical Lutheran Church in America						
The American Lutheran Church					$113,645,260	$73.28
American Lutheran Church	$50,163,078	$73.52	$51,898,875	$74.49		
The Evangelical Lutheran Church	$49,488,063	$65.56	$51,297,348	$66.85		
United Evangelical Lutheran Church	Not Reported: YACC 1961, p. 273		Not Reported: YACC 1963, p. 273			
Lutheran Free Church	$3,354,270	$61.20	$3,618,418	$63.98	$4,316,925	$73.46
Evangelical Lutheran Churches,Assn of	Not Reported: YACC 1961, p. 273		Not Reported: YACC 1963, p. 273			
Lutheran Church in America						
United Lutheran Church	$114,458,260	$68.29	$119,447,895	$70.86	$128,850,845	$76.18
General Council Evang Luth Ch						
General Synod of Evan Luth Ch						
United Syn Evang Luth South						
American Evangelical Lutheran Ch	$1,033,907	$63.83	$1,371,600	$83.63	$1,209,752	$74.89
Augustana Lutheran Church	$31,279,335	$76.97	$33,478,865	$80.88	$37,863,105	$89.37
Finnish Lutheran Ch (Suomi Synod)	$1,685,342	$68.61	$1,860,481	$76.32	$1,744,550	$70.60
Moravian Church in America, No. Prov.	$2,398,565	$89.28	$2,252,536	$82.95	$2,489,930	$90.84
Presbyterian Church (U.S.A.)						
United Presbyterian Ch in U.S.A.	$259,679,057	$82.30	$270,233,943	$84.31	$285,380,476	$87.90
Presbyterian Ch in the U.S.A.						
United Presbyterian Ch in N.A.						
Presbyterian Church in the U.S.	$88,404,631	$99.42	$91,582,428	$101.44	$96,637,354	$105.33
Reformed Church in America	$22,970,935	$103.23	$23,615,749	$104.53	$25,045,773	$108.80
Southern Baptist Convention	$453,338,720	$53.88	$480,608,972	$55.68	$501,301,714	$50.24
United Church of Christ						
Congregational Christian	$100,938,267	$71.12	$104,862,037	$73.20	$105,871,158	$73.72
Congregational						
Evangelical and Reformed	$65,541,874	$80.92	$62,346,084	$76.58	$65,704,662	$80.33
Evangelical Synod of N.A./German						
Reformed Church in the U.S.						
The United Methodist Church						
The Evangelical United Brethren	$47,760,877 e	$64.10	$48,772,149	$65.28	$50,818,912	$68.12
The Methodist Church	$532,854,842 e	$53.97	$553,951,102	$55.14	$581,504,618	$57.27
Methodist Episcopal Church						
Methodist Episcopal Ch South						
Methodist Protestant Church						
Total	$2,127,026,579		$2,214,409,136		$2,365,114,612	

d The 1961 YACC, pa. 273 indicates that this data is not comparable.
e The Evangelical United Brethren and The Methodist Church data is calculated from available data.

Appendix B-3.2: Church member Giving for Eleven Denominations, 1953-1967 (continued)

	Data Year 1962		Data Year 1963		Data Year 1964	
	Total Contributions	Per Capita Total Contributions	Total Contributions	Per Capita Total Contributions	Total Contributions	Per Capita Total Contributions
American Baptist (Northern)	$105,667,332	$68.42	$99,001,651	$68.34	$104,699,557	$69.99
Christian Ch (Disciples of Christ)	$91,889,457	$67.20	$96,607,038	$75.81	$102,102,840	$86.44
Church of the Brethren	$14,594,572	$77.88	$14,574,688	$72.06	$15,221,162	$76.08
The Episcopal Church	$155,971,264	$69.80	$171,125,464	$76.20	$175,374,777	$76.66
Evangelical Lutheran Church in America						
The American Lutheran Church	$114,912,112	$72.47	$136,202,292	$81.11	$143,687,165	$83.83
American Lutheran Church						
The Evangelical Lutheran Church						
United Evangelical Luth. Church						
Lutheran Free Church	$4,765,138	$78.68				
Evangelical Luth. Churches,Assn of						
Lutheran Church in America	$185,166,857	$84.98	$157,423,391	$71.45	$170,012,096	$76.35
United Lutheran Church						
General Council Evang Luth Ch						
General Synod of Evan Luth Ch						
United Syn Evang Luth South						
American Evangelical Luth. Ch						
Augustana Lutheran Church						
Finnish Luth. Ch (Suomi Synod)						
Moravian Church in Am., No. Prov.	$2,512,133	$91.92	$2,472,273	$89.29	$2,868,694	$103.54
Presbyterian Church (U.S.A.)						
United Presbyterian Ch in U.S.A.	$288,496,652	$88.08	$297,582,313	$90.46	$304,833,435	$92.29
Presbyterian Ch in the U.S.A.						
United Presbyterian Ch in N.A.						
Presbyterian Church in the U.S.	$99,262,431	$106.96	$102,625,764	$109.46	$108,269,579	$114.61
Reformed Church in America	$25,579,443	$110.16	$26,918,484	$117.58	$29,174,103	$126.44
Southern Baptist Convention	$540,811,457	$53.06	$556,042,694	$53.49	$591,587,981	$55.80
United Church of Christ	$164,858,968	$72.83	$162,379,019	$73.12	$169,208,042	$75.94
Congregational Christian						
Congregational						
Evangelical and Reformed						
Evangelical Synod of N.A./German						
Reformed Church in the U.S.						
The United Methodist Church						
The Evangelical United Brethren	$54,567,962	$72.91	$49,921,568	$67.37	$56,552,783	$76.34
The Methodist Church	$599,081,561	$58.53	$613,547,721	$59.60	$608,841,881	$59.09
Methodist Episcopal Church						
Methodist Episcopal Ch South						
Methodist Protestant Church						
Total	$2,448,137,339		$2,486,424,360		$2,582,434,095	

NOTE: Data for the years 1965 through 1967 was not available in a form that could be readily analyzed for the present purposes, and therefore data for 1965-1967 was estimated as described in the introductory comments to Appendix B. See Appendix B-1 for 1968-1991 data except for The Episcopal Church and The United Methodist Church, available data for which is presented in the continuation of Appendix B-3 in the table immediately following.

Appendix B-3.3: Church Member Giving for Eleven Denominations, The Episcopal Church and The United Methodist Church, 1968-1995

The Episcopal Church

Data Year	Total Contributions	Full/Confirmed Membership
1968	$194,057,895	2,260,950
1969	$198,728,675	2,238,538
1970	$248,702,969	2,208,773
1971	$257,523,469	2,143,557
1972	$270,245,645	2,099,896
1973	$287,937,285 c	2,084,845 c
1974	$305,628,925	2,069,793
1975	$352,243,222	2,051,964
1976	$375,942,065	2,021,057
1977	$401,814,395	2,114,638
1978	$430,116,564	1,975,234
1979	$484,211,412	1,962,062
1980	$507,315,457	1,933,487
1981	$697,816,298	1,930,690
1982	$778,184,068	1,922,205
1983	$876,844,252	1,906,618
1984	$939,796,743	1,896,056
1985	$1,043,117,983	1,881,250
1986	$1,134,455,479	1,756,120
1987	$1,181,378,441	1,741,036
1988	$1,209,378,098	1,725,581
1989	$1,309,243,747	1,714,122
1990	$1,377,794,610	1,698,240
1991	$1,433,467,803	1,615,505
1992	$1,582,457,015 d	1,614,081 d
1993	$1,613,697,551	1,570,444
1994	$1,696,658,859 d	1,577,996 d
1995	$1,822,460,310	1,585,930

The United Methodist Church

Data Year	Total Contributions	Full/Confirmed Membership
1968	$763,000,434 a	10,849,375 b
1969	$800,425,000	10,671,774
1970	$819,945,000	10,509,198
1971	$843,103,000	10,334,521
1972	$885,708,000	10,192,265
1973	$935,723,000	10,063,046
1974	$1,009,760,804	9,957,710
1975	$1,081,080,372	9,861,028
1976	$1,162,828,991	9,785,534
1977	$1,264,191,548	9,731,779
1978	$1,364,460,266	9,653,711
1979	$1,483,481,986	9,584,771
1980	$1,632,204,336	9,519,407
1981	$1,794,706,741	9,457,012
1982	$1,931,796,533	9,405,164
1983	$2,049,437,917	9,291,936
1984	$2,211,306,198	9,266,853
1985	$2,333,928,274	9,192,172
1986	$2,460,079,431	9,124,575
1987	$2,573,748,234	9,055,145
1988	$2,697,918,285	8,979,139
1989	$2,845,998,177	8,904,824
1990	$2,967,535,538	8,853,455
1991	$3,099,522,282	8,789,101
1992	$3,202,700,721 d	8,726,951 d
1993	$3,303,255,279	8,646,595
1994	$3,430,351,778	8,584,125
1995	$3,568,540,217	8,538,662

[a] The Evangelical United Brethren Data Not Reported: YACC 1970, p. 198-200. This figure is the sum of The Methodist Church in 1968, and the Evangelical United Brethren data for 1967.

[b] This membership figure is an average of the sum of 1967 membership for The Methodist Church and the Evangelical United Brethren and 1969 data for The United Methodist Church.

[c] The Episcopal Church did not report financial data in the 1970 YACC (pp. 198-200) or the 1975 YACC (p. 236). The 1968 dollar figure is prorated based on 1964 and 1969 data for The Episcopal Church. The 1973 dollar figure is an average of 1972 and 1974 data for The Episcopal Church.

[d] Data obtained directly from denominational source.

Appendix B-4: Trends in Giving and Membership

Appendix B-4.1: Membership for Seven Denominations, 1968-1995

Year	American Baptist Churches (Total Memb)	Assemblies of God	Baptist General Conference	Christian and Missionary Alliance	Church of God (Cleveland, TN)	Roman Catholic Church	Salvation Army
1968	1,583,560	610,946	100,000	71,656	243,532	47,468,333	329,515
1969	1,528,019	626,660	101,226	70,573	257,995	47,872,089	331,711
1970	1,472,478	625,027	103,955	71,708	272,276	48,214,729	326,934
1971	1,562,636	645,891	108,474	73,547	287,099	48,390,990	335,684
1972	1,484,393	679,813	111,364	77,991	297,103	48,460,427	358,626
1973	1,502,759	700,071	109,033	77,606	313,332	48,465,438	361,571
1974	1,579,029	751,818	111,093	80,412	328,892	48,701,835	366,471
1975	1,603,033	785,348	115,340	83,628	343,249	48,881,872	384,817
1976	1,593,574	898,711	117,973	83,978	365,124	49,325,752	380,618
1977	1,584,517	939,312	120,222	88,763	377,765	49,836,176	396,238
1978	1,589,610	932,365	131,000	88,903	392,551	49,602,035	414,035
1979	1,600,521	958,418	126,800	96,324	441,385	49,812,178	414,659
1980	1,607,541	1,064,490	133,385	106,050	435,012	50,449,842	417,359
1981	1,621,795	1,103,134	127,662	109,558	456,797	51,207,579	414,999
1982	1,637,099	1,119,686	129,928	112,745	463,992	52,088,774	419,475
1983	1,620,153	1,153,935	131,594	117,501	493,904	52,392,934	428,046
1984	1,559,683	1,189,143	131,162	120,250	505,775	52,286,043	420,971
1985	1,576,483	1,235,403	130,193	123,602	521,061	52,654,908	427,825
1986	1,568,778	1,258,724	132,546	130,116	536,346	52,893,217	432,893
1987	1,561,656	1,275,146	136,688	131,354	551,632	53,496,862	434,002
1988	1,548,573	1,275,148	134,396	133,575	566,917	54,918,949	433,448
1989	1,535,971	1,266,982	135,125	134,336	582,203	57,019,948	445,566
1990	1,527,840	1,298,121	133,742	138,071	620,393	58,568,015	445,991
1991	1,534,078	1,324,800	134,717	141,077	646,201	58,267,424	446,403
1992	1,538,710	1,337,321	134,658	142,346	672,008	59,220,723	450,028
1993	1,516,505	1,340,400	134,814	147,367	700,517	59,858,042	450,312
1994	1,507,934	1,354,337	135,128	147,560	722,541	60,190,605	443,246
1995	1,517,400	1,377,320	135,008	147,955	753,230	60,280,454	453,150

Note regarding American Baptist Churches in the U.S.A. Total Membership data: Total Membership is used for the American Baptist Churches in the U.S.A. for analyses that consider membership as a percentage of U.S. population. The ABC denominational ofice is the source for this data in the years 1968 and from 1986 through 1992. The year 1969 is an average of the years 1968 and 1970. The year 1978 Total Membership data figure is a *YACC* adjusted figure.

Appendix C: Income and Deflators

Appendix C presents U.S. Per Capita Disposable Personal Income for 1921 through 1995.
The Implicit Price Index for Gross National Product is provided for 1921 through 1995. The series keyed to 1992 dollars provided deflators only from 1929 through 1995. Therefore, the 1921 through 1928 data was converted to inflation-adjusted 1958 dollars using the series keyed to 1958=100, and the inflation-adjusted 1958 dollar values were then converted to inflation-adjusted 1992 dollars using the series keyed to 1992 dollars. Biennial Consumer Price Index data for 1987 through 1995 is also listed.

SOURCES
Income 1921-1928, and Deflator 1921-1928

Historical Statistics of the United States: Colonial Times to 1970 Bicentennial Edition, Part 1 (Washington, DC: Bureau of the Census, 1975):

1921-28 Per Capita Disposable Personal Income: Series F 9, p. 224 (F 6-9).

1921-28 Implicit Price Index GNP (1958=100): Series F 9, p. 224 (F 6-9).

Income 1929-1958

Per Capita Disposable Personal Income in Current Dollars: U.S. Department of Commerce, Bureau of Economic Analysis, Personal Income Division: Four-page fax dated Tuesday, June 17, 1997, 02:44 pm from James Rankin.

Income 1959-1990

Per Capita Disposable Personal Income in Current Dollars: U.S. Department of Commerce, Bureau of Economic Analysis, Personal Income Division: Four-page fax dated Monday, June 16, 1997, 04:10 pm from James Rankin.

Income 1991-1994

Per Capita Disposable Personal Income in Current Dollars: U.S. Bureau of Economic Analysis, *Survey of Current Business*, May 1997, Table 8.3, p. 52.

Income 1995

Per Capita Disposable Personal Income in Current Dollars: U.S. Bureau of Economic Analysis, *Survey of Current Business*, May 1997, Table 8.3, p. D-25.

Deflator in 1992 Dollars, 1929-1995

Gross National Product: Implicit Price Deflators for Gross National Product: U.S. Bureau of Economic Analysis, *Survey of Current Business*, May 1997, Table 3, p. 22.

Consumer Price Index [1982-84 = 100]

Monthly Labor Review, Bureau of Labor Statistics (Washington, DC: U.S. Government Printing Office): 1987, 1989 and 1991: July 1993, p. 100; 1993: July 1995, p. 122; 1995: January 1997, p. 108.

Appendix C: Per Capita Disposable Personal Income and Deflators, 1921-1995

Year	Current $s Per Capita Disposable Personal Income	Implicit Price Deflator GNP [1958= 100]	Implicit Price Deflator GNP [1992= 100]
1921	$555	54.5	
1922	$548	50.1	
1923	$623	51.3	
1924	$626	51.2	
1925	$630	51.9	
1926	$659	51.1	
1927	$650	50.0	
1928	$643	50.8	
1929	$680		13.12
1930	$602		12.65
1931	$515		11.34
1932	$390		10.02
1933	$363		9.74
1934	$414		10.28
1935	$461		10.47
1936	$520		10.59
1937	$554		11.04
1938	$506		10.72
1939	$539		10.61
1940	$575		10.76
1941	$697		11.50
1942	$872		12.35
1943	$982		13.02
1944	$1,062		13.36
1945	$1,077		13.72
1946	$1,136		15.38
1947	$1,185		17.10
1948	$1,297		18.10
1949	$1,272		18.10
1950	$1,382		18.29
1951	$1,492		19.60
1952	$1,545		19.94
1953	$1,617		20.19
1954	$1,625		20.41
1955	$1,710		20.75
1956	$1,794		21.47
1957	$1,859		22.18
1958	$1,892		22.72
1959	$1,975		22.96

Year	Current $s Per Capita Disposable Personal Income	Implicit Price Deflator GNP [1992= 100]	CPI
1960	$2,013	23.28	
1961	$2,066	23.55	
1962	$2,156	23.85	
1963	$2,229	24.13	
1964	$2,389	24.49	
1965	$2,546	24.97	
1966	$2,720	25.68	
1967	$2,882	26.50	
1968	$3,101	27.66	
1969	$3,302	28.96	
1970	$3,550	30.50	
1971	$3,811	32.08	
1972	$4,082	33.44	
1973	$4,562	35.32	
1974	$4,941	38.49	
1975	$5,383	42.11	
1976	$5,856	44.58	
1977	$6,383	47.46	
1978	$7,123	50.92	
1979	$7,888	55.26	
1980	$8,697	60.36	
1981	$9,601	66.05	
1982	$10,145	70.21	
1983	$10,803	73.20	
1984	$11,929	75.97	
1985	$12,629	78.57	
1986	$13,289	80.62	
1987	$13,896	83.09	113.6
1988	$14,905	86.12	
1989	$15,789	89.75	124.0
1990	$16,721	93.63	
1991	$17,242	97.33	136.2
1992	$18,113	100.00	
1993	$18,615	102.61	144.5
1994	$19,298	104.94	
1995	$20,214	107.58	152.4

254.8
5797
1995

98043

LINCOLN CHRISTIAN COLLEGE AND SEMINARY

3 4711 00151 2336